# THE BOOK OF MY LIFE

## PHUNG MAI T. CONGTANG

# THE BOOK OF MY LIFE

## PHUNG MAI T. CONGTANG

2024

Copyright © 2024 by Phùng Mai T. CôngTằng

All rights reserved.

Paperback ISBN: 9798321188392
Hardcover ISBN: 9798321255094

No part of this publication may be reproduced, distributed, or transmitted in any form or by any means, including photocopying, recording, or other electronic or mechanical methods, without the prior written permission of the publisher, except as permitted by U.S. copyright law. For permission requests, contact by email at nicknguyen3@gmail.com.

For privacy reasons, some names, locations, and dates may have been changed.

Book Cover by Nicholas Nguyen and Valerie Nguyen. PDF v0.1

First Edition

Illustrations by Various

# DEDICATIONS

TO MY PARENTS
…whose virtue and charity had secured me a lucky and happy life, I respectfully and lovingly dedicate this book as a token of my gratitude.

TO MY BROTHERS, SISTERS, NEPHEWS, AND NIECES
…who always reserve for me a warm and special treatment.

TO DR. ĐỆ T. TÔN, MY DEAR HUSBAND
…who is the source of my happiness, my lifelong collaborator, who taught me Chinese characters, and edited my writings from my doctoral thesis to my poetic works, I dedicate this book as a token of my eternal love.

TO ALL MY CHILDREN AND GRANDCHILDREN
…who are the pride and delight of my life, I dedicate this work in appreciation of your independence, altruism, generosity, and piety.

TO MY TEACHERS,
…whose support and encouragement had tremendously facilitated my college and post-graduate education.

TO MY FRIENDS
…who have somewhat spoiled me and around whom I always feel happy and special.

TO GINNY DOUGLAS, JOHN, TÚ ANH, TÚ TI, AND PV KHA
…who helped me edit this book and whose advice and support gave me inspiration to write about my life.

TO MY DAUGHTER, EMMY TON-SAHIOUNI
…who had spent her precious time to type the manuscript and expedite the publication of this book.

TO THE AMERICAN VICE CONSUL OF VIỆT NAM IN APRIL 1975

...I dedicate this work as proof of my profound gratitude. Following this Vice Consul's advice "To help the poor Americans", I am donating part of the sale revenue of this book to the homeless of Las Vegas via Reverend C.

TO MY SISTER PHÙNG KHÁNH, AKA SƯ CÔ TRÍ HAI

...I am expressing my respect and admiration for her sacrifice to the Buddhist cause and social welfare. I wish to donate part of the income generated by this book to the Vietnamese orphans and indigent, elderly people.

# CONTENTS

**CHAPTER I.** ...................................................................................2
*THE WILLOW FIELD - VỸ DẠ AND MY ORIGIN*

**CHAPTER II.** ..................................................................................8
*THE PRE-SCHOOL YEARS*

**CHAPTER III.** ................................................................................11
*THE FIRST TIME I LEARNED ABOUT DEATH*

**CHAPTER IV.** ................................................................................14
*MOVING TO QUẢNG ĐIỀN AND LEAVING VỸ DẠ*

**CHAPTER V.** .................................................................................27
*BACK TO VỸ DẠ FOR THE FIRST TIME*

**CHAPTER VI.** ................................................................................30
*MOVING TO PHAN THIẾT*

**CHAPTER VII.** ...............................................................................41
*BACK TO VỸ DẠ THE SECOND TIME*

**CHAPTER VIII.** ..............................................................................43
*MY IDLE TIME*

**CHAPTER IX.** ................................................................................55
*BACK TO SCHOOL*

**CHAPTER X.** .................................................................................62
*PRE-MED AND MEDICAL SCHOOL*

**CHAPTER XI.** ................................................................................71
*WORKING AT HUẾ GENERAL HOSPITAL*

**CHAPTER XII.** ...............................................................................75
*MY EXPERIENCE IN B'LAO HOSPITAl*

**CHAPTER XIII**......................................................................80

*MY PRIVATE PRACTICE IN QUI NHƠN*

**CHAPTER XIV.** ...................................................................84

*THE RETREAT TO THE SOUTH- VIA NHA TRANG, PHAN RANG, PHAN THIẾT, AND VŨNG TÀU*

**CHAPTER XV.** ....................................................................95

*THE REUNION IN VŨNG TÀU*

**CHAPTER XVI.** ...................................................................98

*GOING TO SÀI GÒN AND FINDING A WAY TO LEAVE VIỆT NAM*

**CHAPTER XVII.** ................................................................109

*ON THE WAY OUT OF VIỆT NAM AND LIVING AS REFUGEES*

**CHAPTER XVIII.** ...............................................................114

*SETTLING IN THE UNITED STATES, WILMOT, ARKANSAS*

**CHAPTER XIX.** .................................................................119

*MOVING TO MICHIGAN AND STARTING RESIDENCY IN PSYCHIATRY*

**CHAPTER XX.** ..................................................................128

*STARTING RESIDENCY IN CHILD AND ADOLESCENT PSYCHIATRY*

**CHAPTER XXI.** .................................................................132

*RELOCATED IN OHIO*

**CHAPTER XXII.**.................................................................134

*MOVING TO LAS VEGAS, NEVADA*

**EXHIBIT A** .......................................................................142

*EXHIBIT A*

**EXHIBIT B** .......................................................................144

*EXHIBIT B*

**EXHIBIT C**.......................................................................145

*EXHIBIT C*

**EXHIBIT D** ................................................................................ **147**
    *EXHIBIT D*

**EXHIBIT E** ................................................................................ **149**
    *EXHIBIT E*

# CHAPTER I.

## THE WILLOW FIELD - VỸ DẠ AND MY ORIGIN

I grew up in a small village named Vỹ Dạ,[1] which stands for the "Willow Field," situated in the outskirts of Huế, the ancient capital of Việt Nam. Vỹ Dạ was chosen by my great-grandfather, the Viceroy Tuy Lý[2] to establish his very large family and children. My great-grandfather was the eleventh son of Emperor Minh Mạng, the successor of Emperor Gia Long, the founder of the last dynasty of Vietnam; the Nguyễn Phước Dynasty (1802-1953).

I was born in my grandparents' home, nestled on the right bank of Sông Hương, the Perfume River, and built behind the monument to Viceroy Tuy Lý. My great-grandfather, Viceroy Tuy Lý, was also a famous poet, and Vỹ Dạ was named after his pen name. My birth coincided with the first blossoming of our precious ornamental white plum tree in the front yard. Accordingly, my paternal aunt gave me my first name Phùng Mai meaning "meeting the Plum Flower." This name gave me a few troubles in school because it can be distorted by kids to sound like "phồng mang" in Vietnamese which means "expand your neck like a cobra."

[1] Pronounced *Veya*
[2] Pronounced *Tweelee*

Near the white plum tree, on the right side of our family home, was a lotus pond where I used to play in the water while smelling the lotus flowers. I still remember watching the fish swim in the pond during summertime.

It was 1932, and I was the fifth child born to three brothers and one sister. Since I was the baby of the family for seven years, I was the *chou-chou* of my father. My brother, Đích[3] who is three years my elder, used to tease me "You have three great positions; the Last Born, the Favorite, and the Modern Girl of daddy." In turn, he was the favorite of my mother. I became a big sister too, as later my three younger sisters were born.

I have yet to include two older brothers as well, who I unfortunately never met, because they tragically passed away from childhood illnesses before I was born. One died from cholera and another from dysentery. My older brother who died from dysentery I suspect was killed by the treatments of our family doctor who gave him Santonin and Calomel, an arsenic product to purge the roundworms. I found this out because this same family doctor had later caused the death of my younger sister, Phùng Hảo, with the same treatment when she was three years old with bacterial dysentery. These early experiences taught me the importance of sound medical decisions. I was eleven years old when Phùng Hảo died. When she died, she was lying in her crib at home and said to my mother and her wet nurse who were at her side, "Mommy, I am dying, Mụ Vú[4] I am dying," before she closed her eyes forever.

My father lost his own father at an early age. There was rumor that his father committed suicide. My paternal grandmother shaved her head like a nun at age 40 after her husband's death. She was a beautiful woman and by shaving her head, she wanted to prove to

---

[3] Pronounced *Dick*
[4] Pronounced *Moovoo*, this was what she called her wet nurse.

herself and others that she would stay single to raise her children. She was very erudite in Chinese characters, being the daughter of Ông Ích Khiêm, a famous warrior at the time. When I was growing up, I used to see many Buddhist monks and famous people come to consult my grandmother about Chinese characters and poems. She read Chinese books and Buddhist texts daily until she died at age 85 in 1954.

My father was an educator who studied both Chinese and French. He specialized in French dictionaries and phonetics. He loved Vietnamese classical music and my mother had to serve his music teachers who stayed with the family for many consecutive months. He was a fine man and a caring teacher. Thousands of his students still respect and love him.

My mother is the next to the youngest daughter of Đặng Liên, who was the royal physician and father-in-law to the contemporary Emperor Khải Định. My mother's second sister was married to the Emperor when he was still named the "Oldest Prince". My aunt later separated from the emperor and returned home to live with my grandfather. She was very close to my parents and adopted my eldest sister, Khánh Trợ. Khánh Trợ was named so because that she was born when my father was a teacher in Khánh Hòa province.

My mother lost her own mother when she was four years old. Before my grandmother died, she recommended her best friend to marry her husband and take care of her children. Thus, we have a step-maternal grandmother who was a devoted Buddhist. In her old age, she resided at Tường Vân Temple (Benevolent Cloud). Tường Vân is the temple where the Buddhist President Thích Tịnh Khiết resided for almost 80 years until he passed away. I am very proud of my Buddhist origin because I am a disciple of Thích Tịnh Khiết and my sisters, cousin, and aunt, are Buddhist nuns.

My mother was a very strong and intelligent woman. She was raised by her father and step-mother. She did not go to school because most of the Vietnamese women of her generation stayed home and married. She did try to study at home, but she didn't have enough time due to her duties as a wife, mother, and daughter-in-law. She used to say, "A woman who has a husband is just like a man who has a career and a position in society."

During her time, fulfilling the obligations of a daughter-in-law was a very important matter for a Vietnamese girl. If she was not loved by her husband's family, especially his parents and siblings, she could be divorced without protest.

My mother struggled to please my father's big sister. Divorce during this time was a disgrace to the family. She often had to swallow her anger and pride and endure the injustices and false accusations of my father's siblings to keep her family intact. For the first ten years of her marriage, my father gave all his salary to his mother to manage the household. My paternal grandmother was a widow at that time and had three minor children to raise although she did stop receiving my father's salary when all her younger children moved out to marry or start careers.

Although self-educated, my mother appeared smarter than my father. She had embedded in her children many principles of conduct. My oldest brother respected her like a "saint". I would apply her teaching in my everyday life.

She used to teach by quoting sayings and proverbs selected from the "Precious Book to Have an Enlightened Conscience". This book is in Chinese characters which uses a few words to mean lots of things. I applied her teaching to be generous, charitable, and industrious. Her teachings protected me from worrying about the future and from holding a grudge.

Among the lessons she would teach us:

*"Distribute generously your favors and caring, you will meet many good friends anywhere. Don't make casual enemies or you might later encounter them in some difficult situation…"*

*"Do helpful things every day and you will develop a charitable heart" or again "if you do and think the right things now, you don't have to worry about your or your children's future…"*

*"When you know you have enough of everything, you live in peace and harmony. When you don't yearn for anything, you can feel the real pride…"*

Where I disagreed with my mother was that she loved and respected her male children over her female children. I noticed her bias and I protested, "Why? Because Buddha is a man? But we have a female Buddha, too!" My mother used to scold me, "You are a girl, you should not do this or that." To which I often replied "Why not? My brother Đích can do it without a problem. Girls, aren't they human beings?" Sometimes I would get a spanking by my oldest brother for talking back to my mother and my mother continued to discriminate against girls.

When I was a teenager, I lost my third brother, Bửu Đà, during the military war. My brother at 23 years old, became a national hero and received a posthumous award that read "The Nation Acknowledges Your Good Deed." He was my mother's favorite child, and he was very fond of me. I was his "protégée" and my brother Đích was his "enemy" because Đích criticized him sarcastically, "You are a grown-up and you are still Mama's parasite!"

After the death of my brother, Bửu Đà, I received a new "weapon" to challenge my mother's discrimination. I told her my unkind observation, "You had five sons, and you favor them so much that three of them died. You have not learned a lesson yet! When you grow old, who will take care of you; your sons, or your daughters?" After that time, I believe my mother understood her unfairness.

I finally confronted my mother about her bias against her daughters, and she explained, "Because my life as a girl and a woman were so hard and unsatisfactory, that's why I wanted to give birth to all boys who would have a better life." I suggested, "If it was correct what you believed, you should love your daughters more!"

She responded with a metaphor, "Women are like stray boats, they have dozens of places to drift and would be blessed if the water is clean; and be damned if the water is filthy!"

I refused to accept this and retorted, "No way! I will choose the man I marry. I will contribute and build my destiny. I will study hard, go to college, and become a useful, respectable person in society!" In the early 40s, this was a time barely ten years since Việt Nam's first female doctor[5] started practicing. However, inspired by my mother's deep reverence for doctors, Buddhist monks, and teachers... I chose to pursue a career in medicine.

---

[5] Dr Henriette Bùi Quang Chiêu started practicing in 1934 (1906–2012)

## CHAPTER II.

### THE PRE-SCHOOL YEARS

I was a very verbal child. When I started to talk, my family would teach me nursery rhymes and Buddhist liturgy. By the time I was four years old, my sister Khánh Trợ and my father used to teach me Vietnamese, French and Chinese poems. I would recite these liturgies and poems to my grandmother's guests and receive lots of applause and awards. I used to get money as prizes and my father would hold me up to put the money in his iron safe to keep it for me. I have no recall that I ever got those savings back, but sometimes my father would sign a piece of paper for me to get candies or cookies at my aunt's shop. My aunt would add up these credits and cash them at the end of each month.

I was so good at reciting Buddhist liturgy that my aunt, Mrs. Ưng Úy called me her "talking bird." My aunt was highly respected because her father, her husband, and brother are all ministers. Her husband, my uncle, was Ưng Úy the Minister of Education at the time and their son was Professor Bửu Hội, a famous scientist and diplomat. My aunt was very fond of me and would send her servants to bring me delicacies and instructed that they always refer to me as "her talking bird."

I was very eager to learn in kindergarten, I was the teacher's pet. I would hang around the older students and play or rock in the teacher's hammock when they were reading their primary spelling books aloud in unison. I listened to all their lessons and tried to memorize everything they learned. During lunch break, I would follow the older students to go fishing in the swamp or rice paddy fields. The students would catch fish, shrimps, crabs, and frogs to give to the teacher.

My family used to laugh when telling stories about my willfulness in kindergarten. My live-in babysitter would walk or piggyback me to school. One afternoon, I refused to be picked up by my babysitter because the teacher had an anniversary offering to his ancestors. I told my babysitter, "No, I don't want to go home now. I want to pay respect to the deceased first." Then I pleaded to my teacher, "Please, let me pay respect to your ancestor, no eating is OK with me." The teacher then gave me a treat to take home before the ceremony started.

At this age, I started to use my wits to get out of trouble. My grandmother has a garden full of fruit trees. My favorite fruit is the Bonanza fruit meaning "plentiful wishes". My grandmother used to pick them when they were nearly ripe because the birds would eat them if they were soft on the trees. She used to keep them in a big rice jar. I would pick the best from the tree to exchange for a ripe one when my grandmother was not around. Once, she saw me eating her fruit when she was chewing something. She spit it out in a hurry to scold me. I replied with a rhyme, "You are spitting, I am eating, we are even." (Bà Nội nhổ ba trầu, Phùng Mai ăn mãn cầu, tụi mình huề!) and she said nothing but laughed.

My mother reported that I was a vindictive but logical child. Since my grandmother was a Buddhist, we could not kill living animals. Once my mother told a servant to go buy live escargots when my grandmother was away from home. They cooked and ate them and did not give me as much as I wanted. I threatened to tell grandmother when she returned, and when I did, my mother denied it. In a huff, I went to the garden and brought in a few escargot shells as evidence. My mother claimed they were old shells that were cooked a long time ago. I would not give up and affirmed, "If you give a toothpick, I will give you the living proof from my mouth!" The whole family laughed.

# CHAPTER III.

## THE FIRST TIME I LEARNED ABOUT DEATH

My grandmother coughed up blood occasionally since her forties. She always worried about her health and bought a coffin early on made of precious wood. She also had a cottage built for herself adjacent to our large brick house. She would not keep the coffin in her cottage but placed it in our house instead. I grew up with the coffin as a mainstay in our large family room. I was not afraid of the coffin and used to hide behind it when we played hide-and-seek. My brother Đích and I were very curious about death. Sometimes we prayed that our grandmother would die so that we could see what death looks like.

I was seven years old when my first younger sister, Phùng Khánh, was born. We hired a wet nurse from a distant village. We knew that the wet nurse had a husband and three children: two girls and one baby boy about three months older than my sister. This boy died before the nurse came to live with us. Our nurse did not want us to know her name or her husband's name. She only wanted to be called "Nurse" (Mụ Vú). She also nursed my late sister, Phùng Hảo, whom I talked about earlier. We were very curious about her name and her family and swore to find out.

One day, when we were playing in the front yard, a man and two women appeared at the gate. We could tell by their clothes and dark complexion that they came from the country. We ran out and asked them about her nurse. It turned out that they came from our nurse's home as we had guessed. We found out our nurse's name and her husband's name, but we also learned the horrible news that her husband had died two days prior.

When Mụ Vú learned the sad news, she threw herself on the floor, crying, moaning, rolling, and thrashing her arms and legs. She was always calm, cool, happy, and smiling, so it was a shock since I never saw her upset before. After I saw her emotional reaction to her husband's death, I wished that nobody would die because it was too painful to the loving survivors they left behind. From that time on, I felt guilty about my death wish toward my beloved grandmother.

Our nurse lived with us off and on for many years. She raised all my three younger sisters.

We took care of her in her old age, and we helped her family after she passed away.

## ELEMENTARY SCHOOL: FIGHTING WITH THE DOG FOR A CRAB'S BONE

I grew up with a fear of large dogs. This started from a dog bite that I received at nine years old. My brother Đích and I were visiting a cousin who lived behind our house. They were eating steamed crabs while a big dog was waiting under the table for leftovers. I saw two small yellow ducklings running under the table toward the dog. I crawled after them to catch one near the dog. He got mad and bit me on the forearm.

When we went home and told my mother, she asked how it happened. My brother gave her an explanation that was too stupid and funny to be forgotten, "she fought with the dog for a crab's bone, that's why it bit her." My mother had our servant take the dog to the

Pasteur's Institute to test it for rabies. I was taken to the hospital emergency room for preventive rabies shots. The dog happened to die during the test, and I had to receive 21 rabies shots: one each day for the next three weeks.

One day, coming back from the hospital on a bicycle rickshaw, we were about half an hour from my house when we met one of my uncles walking along the street. He asked the driver for a ride, and he was picked up and sat next to me. I was very afraid because allegedly this uncle was "crazy" due to syphilis. Normally, if it wasn't my uncle I would have protested and refused to accept a stranger. But I was so frightened of my uncle that I remained silent. I was afraid that my uncle would bite me like the dog, meaning more shots. The rabies shots were painful due to the volume of the anti-rabies serum (5 ml!), and I received them subcutaneously in my abdomen, around the umbilicus.

Once, my third-grade teacher picked me to stand on the desk to sing the French national anthem for the class, but I was in tears because it hurt where I took the injections. It was a surprise for everybody to see the happy-go-lucky little girl, who was always ready to sing or to recite La Fontaine's Fables, crying when she got picked.

# CHAPTER IV.

## MOVING TO QUẢNG ĐIỀN AND LEAVING VỸ DẠ

My father was promoted to District Inspector of Education of Quảng Điền. He would supervise all the elementary schools in the Quảng Điền District.

### MEMORIES OF VỸ DẠ

I was sad to leave Vỹ Dạ because we would leave behind all the splendor of my childhood. Vỹ Dạ was famous for its many beautiful houses, courtyards, fancy brick and iron walls and street porches. Most of my great-uncles were high class mandarins of the royal court and they decorated their residence and villas with good taste. Some of them had a small zoo in the front yard with different species of birds, parakeets, peacocks, pheasants, monkeys, etc... I used to get chased by the geese when I came to visit the animals. Other houses were distinguished by their beautiful flowers and bonsai trees. The houses located by the river side would have neat concrete steps going down to the river.

My parents had a house by the Perfume River, and we had a large tree many hundreds of years old, leaning over the river. Its large superficial roots would serve as steps. We used to climb up the tree and jump down the river from its branches. During summertime, many families would build floating cottages above the river. All the families would build a big communal floating cottage and many people would go there to have parties, play music, read poems, swim, fish, and have a good time. Two or three times per year we had ceremonies when we would float colorful paper lanterns on the water while setting the fish free in the river. Sometimes we also set the birds free during these occasions.

There were anniversary ceremonies when we had to kill three animals to offer to the deceased. Any time when I noticed a cow and a goat tied in a corner of my garden, adjacent to Viceroy Tuy Lý's temple, I knew that we would have a great feast and treat! These animals appeared kind of sad, though. The third animal to be sacrificed was a large pig. As a custom, the families had to offer livestock, instead of meat from the market. A butcher was hired to prepare the meat. A special cook would roast the whole pork over charcoal. They would put seasoning inside the pork and stuff it with lemongrass and grapefruit leaves. The cook would stand by the whole time during the roasting to put water all over the pork skin with a brush made of fresh banana stems. In this way, the roasted skin would turn golden, soft, and crunchy. I was very interested in watching all the steps in preparing the meals. This was an occasion for all Viceroy Tuy Lý's grand-daughters-in-law and grand-daughters to show their cooking skills.

In my small family, preparing for the anniversary of great grand-father's death would take many weeks. First, we prepare all sorts of pickles, anchovies, and crab caviar paste, etc... Then many sorts of dehydrated cookies were made from sweet rice, mung beans, lima beans, etc... Then when it was close to the anniversary day, steamed sweet treats were made from tapioca, coconut, and lotus seed paste and sugar. Many distinguished guests and relatives would come for the ceremony. Due to this, all the weeks-long prepared foods would be finished in two meals!

It often felt like a big waste of time and labor. However, the women in the family would just spent their time to prepare three meals a day alongside the festival preparation. At that time, they went to the market sometimes twice daily to buy fresh garden vegetables and live shrimps and fish. Because we didn't have freezers or refrigerators at that time, I sometimes kept the uncooked live shrimp or fish as pets. However, they usually died a few days later.

I knew that I would miss Vỹ Dạ when our family moved to Quảng Điền, a smaller village, half a day walk form old Capital Huế.

## MOVING TO QUẢNG ĐIỀN

Quảng Điền means "The Large Rice Fields". We stayed in Quảng Điền for about two years and met with two different district chiefs. The first was Yem who was related to my farther. His wife is my cousin. The second district chief, Tran, was related to my mother. He called my parents' aunt and uncle.

We bought the house of the previous school inspector who was also my uncle. He had pulmonary tuberculosis and my mother had to fumigate the house for three days before we moved in.

Our house was situated next to the district elementary school. The school principal Cao Hữu Hoanh also called my father uncle because he belonged to the group of scholars who came to study Chinese characters with my father. My mother used to give small parties to entertain these "adopted" nephews.

During those times, after finishing third grade, some older students would take an exam called "mandatory comprehensive." After sixth grade, we would take the Primary Examination. In this remote village, these exams were big events. Many villagers wore colorful uniforms while holding red and blue parasols to escorts the arrival or departure of the VIP including the school inspector and the district chief who came to preside over the distribution of certificates. The lucky ones who passed the exam were able to get positions on the village manager board and were generally exempt from free labor.

I was very intrigued by the use of free labor for the community for the uneducated. My mother said, "This is less unfair than the 'body tax' that each Vietnamese adult man had to pay to the French government. That was why many people had to leave their villages and family to labor in French rubber tree plantations to get the money to pay this tax. Most of these men "recruited" by the French never returned home because they would die from paludism in those plantations."

Moving to Quảng Điền, I thought it would be better because my big brother would not follow us. He was the one designated by my mother to spank us. Sometimes I would prepare for the spanking by placing layers of towels inside my pants to lessen the pain. I was disappointed because my mother figured this out and used other tactics and instruments to punish me.

When I disobeyed, she would send a servant to my teacher's house convoking him to come to give me a spanking. Once, I went with the servant to my teacher's house. I saw him eating lunch with his family. He quickly finished his meal to go with us. He did not spank me that time, only giving me some instructions and telling me to apologize.

Afterwards, I promised myself not to provoke my mother to the point she would call my teacher. Around 11 or 12 years old, I already learned the three preconditions to best communicate: best time, best place, and best rapport. I chose a moment when my mother was in a good mood and told her: "Mother, I think it's not fair to make my teacher come anytime you are mad at me. That is not his job. People might think you are using your power and position to manipulate him." My mother seemed to understand and this was one of my early uses of this communication strategy.

One of the behaviors that my mother disapproved of was my association with the water buffalo keepers but despite this I always had a good time with them. They were boys and girls my age, riding on the buffalo's back and guiding them to the grazing fields. They either climbed on the animal's back or held its tail and stepped on its rear knee to get on its back. I did not want to hold the tail and my friends would offer me their holding hands or back to step on. They were very kind to me, always treating me with respect and calling me "Big Sister".

They would show me the good places to pick raspberries and blueberries, where I could find a bird nest, a beehive or plenty of mussels and clams. My brother Đích and I used to go fishing and catching shrimp in the deep fields or the shallow river. After a flood was a crop of small shrimps. We would hold a lantern over the water and the shrimps would gather around the light and we catch them with a small hand net.

## THE DEATH OF THREE STUDENTS: MY ANGER AT THE SUPERSTITIOUS BOAT PEOPLE

One afternoon, when we were swimming, playing, and hunting for clams in the river, we saw three boys our age 12-14 years old, swimming far from the riverbank. One of them went further and hit a deep spot.

He was exhausted and called for help. A boat that was anchoring close to the boy did not move. We all called out for help. The two other boys swam out to help the first one. We shouted "No, no, the boat people should help him!"

No response.

We saw the three boys pulling grabbing at one another and all of them drowned.

There were three adults on the boat. They only needed to hand them a long pole that used to be at hand on the boat to save them. They did not do it because they were afraid that the "ghost of the river" might retaliate and kill their offsprings!

I was incredibly angry at the boat people. I wished that somebody would prosecute the boat owner for letting the boys drown. Nobody did. We went back to the village and talked about the accident. People ran out, using boats, and diving to retrieve the corpses. It took a few hours before they could retrieve all the bodies.

They placed them parallel on the bank. They did some symbolic ceremonies to retrieve their "souls" from the river and reunify them with the bodies before they placed them in the coffins. This accident and injustice made me wish I was a district chief so that I could punish the superstitious inhumane people.

## WE GOT ROBBED

I woke up after midnight, hearing my father calling, "Honey, there is a dog which is scratching the wall. Let him out!" My mom replied, "You were dreaming. there is no dog at all." A short time later, my father said, "Honey, it is a bear, a big bear, I just saw it!"

My mother got up and lit her lamp to prove that my father was wrong. My father used to say funny things to my mother's disapproval. Then she noticed a shirt on the floor. She went to the closet to find all the clothes gone! She then checked the front door and side door. They were locked. Then she looked under my bed and there was a big hole dug by the robber.

She ordered the servants to light up the lamps and beat on the copper pans to alert the villagers. She angrily said, "This robber has lots of guts! He dared to enter and exit through the same hole. He did not bother to open a safe door to escape. He really thought that we are very stupid to act this way, but I will get him!"

In my suspicious mind, I thought my mother really meant that my father was stupid, believing the robber was a dog when he dug the big hole and a bear when held all our clothing in a bear hug. My father's inattentiveness had lost almost all his clothes, but he was not angry, instead he smiled and laughed about his naivete. As always, he would let my mother deal with the incident.

When the villagers came, my mother declared, "I will file a complaint against the village. We are guests in your village, and you did not protect us! When we got robbed, we called for help! And instead, you waited to gather for almost an hour after the robber was gone!" The shamed villagers promised to look for the culprit. At that time, there was a chief in each district who would know who committed crimes in the area or would contact his counterpart in the adjacent districts to find out.

Next morning, the news spread all over the village. The District Chief came to my house to carry out the investigation. The district soldiers took the "footprint" on the crumbling dirt around the hole outside of the house. A few hours later, they brought in a poor man wearing a ragged comic straw hat. This man had Hansen disease also known as Leprosy and lost his fingers and toes. I stood by the District Chief who was standing high on the porch, looking down on the poor man.

The man was arrested based on the footprint found at the scene of the crime. The robber had walked with his toes up to fool the police. The poor man pleaded not guilty, saying" Sir, please do judge with your generous celestial lights to see that I am sick and disabled. Incapable of digging the hole and robbing the Inspector." I thought he was perfectly right and felt so sorry for him when suddenly the Chief said, with his severe and loud tone of voice, "Young man, why are you so impolite? You're still wearing your hat in front of your superior?" The sick man hurriedly used his wrists to take off his hat.

The chief immediately observed, "See? if you can use your hands to take off your hat, you can also use them to take other people's property!" Nevertheless, after making his point and showing his power and authority, he told his soldiers to release the sick man.

A few days later, my mother was notified that the robber had been identified. I went with my mother in a boat with three district soldiers. When we reached the designated village, we came directly to a small house. As we were approaching the front door, I saw a shadow disappearing in a room on the right. Inside, sitting on a low bamboo bed was a very old woman who was almost blind.

Apparently, the robber was sitting with his mother when we came. My mother was touched deeply by the situation and said, "It turns out that he stole to feed his old sick mother!" and she handed some cash to the elderly woman and said, "Tell your son not to steal. He can work to help feed you. I will drop the charge."

The woman cried out of gratitude, "If he is put in prison, I might die. Thank you. I will never forget your benevolent act." Witnessing my mother's determination to catch the thief turn into compassion for his circumstances made me realize that there are always two sides of any story.

My mother inspected the adjacent room and found two large baskets full of our clothes. My mother counted the clothing and only two small shirts were missing. She said, "The missing pieces are the ones the robber threw on the road to distract his chasers!"

## MY MOTHER INVESTIGATED A THEFT

A few months later, my big brother and sister-in-law visited before leaving to shop in Huế. When they returned after a two-week vacation, my mother noticed that my sister was not wearing her gold bracelet. My sister said it was lost. My mother asked when was the last time she saw it on her wrist and when was the first time she noticed it was gone? My sister said, "When I was waiting for the boat to cross the river, it was still there. After we crossed the river, it was lost, and we looked in the boat and could not find it!"

My mother said, "Poor thing, why didn't you tell me right away? Waiting for two weeks, it would be harder to retrieve! Maybe you lost it while waiting on the beach!" Then my mother sent out two servants. One asked the people who saw my brother and sister at the pier what other people were there at the same time. Another servant asked if anyone noticed anything special in the small community during the past two weeks, who came to town, who left town, etc...

The servants returned and reported that they found out that a man was there when my sister dropped the bracelet and that the same man went to town the next day before returning with cash to spend on new clothes and shoes.

My mother brought the police to talk to that man. He confessed that when he saw my sister's bracelet on the ground, he moved to squat over it. When my sister left, he took it, then sold it to a jeweler in town. My mother and two policemen went with him to the jeweler's shop. The jeweler already made a new bracelet out of the old one. The jeweler asked my mother to take it and she did after warning him that it was wrong to buy stolen goods and it was for Buddha's sake that she did not make him replace exactly the same bracelet that he had bought!

## THE DEATH OF MY SISTER, PHÙNG HẢO

My sister was one and a half years old when we moved to Quảng Điền. She was a charming toddler, always pleasant and smiling. I was assigned to give her a daily bath and she would plead each time, "Sister, don't pour water on my head, OK?" She had the same wet nurse who nursed her one-year older sister, Phùng Khánh. Phùng Hảo also had a boy babysitter named "Big Size."

One day, I went with Big Size, taking my sister Phùng Hảo to visit a neighbor who was the concierge of the elementary school. I noticed that one of the concierge's children had had dysentery and passed frequent stools made of blood threaded mucus. A few days later, my sister developed dysentery. My mother and the wet nurse brought her into town to be treated. We were about half a day walk from Huế, but my mother took the boat which would get there in about 10 to 12 hours.

A few days later, I was awakened by a noise that sounded like somebody laughing. I ran to Hoa, my sister-in-law's room. She happened to be staying with us at that time and she had just given birth. I asked if she heard the noise. She looked frightened and said, "Yes, it is the night owl. It brings bad news." At that moment, the owl flew over our house again and went, "Coo, coo, coo..." At first it was slow and distinct, then it went faster and faster and faded into the distance. My sister- in-law, Hoa, told me to pray that nothing bad would happen and I went back to sleep.

About two or three o'clock in the morning we were awakened by a servant who returned from Huế. He cried out before entering the house, "Sister Hoa, our baby sister Phùng Hảo is dead." Sister Hoa was sitting in her bed breast feeding her baby when she learned the horrible news. She rubbed her heels back and forth on the bed, saying "Big Size, you killed my baby sister."

A few weeks later, after the funeral, my parents returned home. I asked my mother what happened in Huế. She said she took my sister to our physician uncle who gave her a prescription to buy medicine to kill round worms. My sister got worse after the treatment and died three days later.

I was very disappointed and furious, "Mother, this doctor has the reputation of giving round worm killer to anybody who has diarrhea or dysentery. Why would you listen to him and follow his prescription? We have Dr. Phan, your niece's husband, on father's side. Why didn't you get his help?"

My mother sadly replied, "You don't know. It's very complicated. If I bought my child to be treated by my family's doctor and something happened, I could not live with your father's family. They would blame it on me and repeat the accusation for the rest of my life."

I was not convinced, "How could you sacrifice your child to please or quiet your in-law? She might not have died if she had a good conscientious doctor!" My mother said, "Let's not talk about this any longer. I am already so hurt. Maybe it was her fate to die at age three. Maybe Buddha wants her back to Nirvana, the everlasting happiness." I was content that my mother's religious belief helped her alleviate her suffering.

## A MURDER ATTEMPT

My parents hired a relative to manage their household. We called him Big Uncle Ben. Uncle Ben would supervise us and the servants. He helped organize small parties to entertain my parents' guests. He made sure that everything in the house was in order.

He was stricter than my mother. He made sure that we brought back the tools, instruments, utensils, and makeshift toys after we played. We did not have toys in our time, so we made our own toys by cutting dolls out of cardboard paper and dressing them with paper dresses or making dolls and doll house, furniture, etc. out of toothpicks. Somehow, I got help to build a large chicken house adjacent to our kitchen. I ended up with 45 chickens in that house, starting with two small ones. I was so successful that my mother was convinced to let me raise a pig. Considering that Buddhist belief is against raising animals which end up getting killed, I knew my mother have loved me a lot to indulge this interest.

One summer day, a male relative came to visit us. We called him Younger Uncle Ngan. Uncle Ngan was very fond of my pig and my chicken coop. He helped me fix the walls to make sure the chicken would be protected from the wind. He asked if he could have two chickens to make soup to treat the whole family. I turned him down because I wanted them to get bigger and reproduce. Uncle Ngan was about 25 years old and had no job. He asked my parents' permission to stay with us a few days. We were very glad because he was fun to play with.

He was very "nice" to old Uncle Ben. He used to buy him beer and wine to my mother's disapproval. So, he started doing it when my mother was not there, asking me not to tell. I didn't mind since Uncle Ben was more relaxed and happier after a drink, often cracking jokes and laughing. He became easier to live with since he was less grouchy and more lenient about making me put away my toys and tools.

One night I was awakened by the sounds of a physical altercation and ran to the family room. I heard somebody screaming, "Help! Help! He is killing me. He stabbed me!" I saw old Uncle Ben crawling and ducking under the table and a shadow of a man dashing toward the door and disappearing into the night. It was young Uncle Ngan who never came back after the incident.

My mother and Mụ Vú came from the big house, bringing petroleum lamps. They looked under the table and found Uncle Ben curled up in the fetal position, shaking like a leaf. His shirt was stained with blood. My mother ordered Mụ Vú to pull him out and sit him on a chair. He took off his shirt and she examined the wounds. With relief, my mother concluded, "It's not very serious, thank God. No vital points were hit. He only used a small knife."

When the knife was mentioned, Mụ Vú said, "A moment ago, I heard somebody moving things in the corner where we keep the big, curved knife to cut wood. I thought the dog was chasing the cat!" Mu Vu went to look for the big knife. "It is not here!" She called out. Good thing that Uncle Ngan didn't use the larger knife to attack Uncle Ben!

Suddenly mention of the big knife jogged my memory. The knife, I said, "It is in the chicken house. I didn't put it back because Uncle Ben was so nice when has a drink!"

My mother asked Uncle Ben, "Why would he want to kill you?" and he answered, "Because I was very strict when I was a butler at his parents' house." Uncle Ben used to threaten the servants with things like, "I will beat you to death! Even inside a pagoda, I wouldn't care." He succeeded in making serious enemies with his morbid threats.

Looking back, Uncle Ngan had the symptoms of an antisocial personality and my mother, as clever as she was, did not suspect because I kept it a secret that he was getting Uncle Ben drunk, which ultimately made it easier for him to carry out the stabbing! But luckily, it was also the reason that it didn't end up being worse!

## CHAPTER V.

### BACK TO VỸ DẠ FOR THE FIRST TIME

We have had enough exciting and sad moments at Quảng Điền. So, when we learned that my father was promoted to school inspector in a large district, I was happy to learn that would mean moving back to Vỹ Dạ!

Little did not know that I would return to a disaster.

My upcoming sixth-grade teacher was… my big brother Minh!

He made me sit on the boys' side to prevent me from being talkative. There were three long desks for girls on the left-hand side and boys on the right. He made me sit on the second desk, on the right-hand side, next to the boys and in full line of sight of his desk! I sat at the end on the side of the middle aisle where he would pace up and down with his long ratan rod.

At the first desk in front of me sat my cousin Bửu Giao who was very smart but neurotic. He used to show me his sweating hand where the sweat dropped from his fingers. Sitting behind me were my two cousins, B. Phieu, and B. Khuong, who was a good singer.

Next to me were two other boys along with N.V. Bách and H.N. Tùng. Bách and Tùng are now doctors. But at that time, my brother used to call us "idiots" and rated us "mediocre," I hated that word.

My brother divided the class into many teams with a team leader for each. Each team will take turns to keep the class clean and in order. The team leader would orchestrate the class routine. All I have learned from my brother were many patriotic songs, maxims, and the qualities of our national heroes. Each morning, the team leader in charge would call out the name of his team's hero and the whole class stated his quality written on the blackboard by the team leader. The leader then designated what song to be sung and who to start the song. After we finished singing, he would allow us to sit down and return to his seat. The leader would repeat the same routine when we left the classroom to go home. We always gathered up our stuff, singing.

My brother used to play his violin for the students. Some of the students still loved and respected him despite his strict spankings… but some didn't. I belonged to the second group. I had continued to receive his spanking until one day when I thought of a scheme.

Unfortunately, his second child, who was a precious boy, had pneumonia and died. I was very sad for him and for our family. I lit a candle and stood in front of a small temple in our garden. I prayed for our family to receive happiness and good health, knowing that my sister-in-law was watching. Then I approached her and said, "Since brother Minh is now married and has children, he can no longer spank me even when Mama orders him to! He has two children and through my prayers, one was already deceased! Has he not learned his lesson yet?"

My sister-in-law was very scared. She promised me that she would pray for her husband to never spank me again. I had succeeded in using her superstition to terminate my ordeal.

From that day on, my brother had stopped spanking me, possibly because he thought I was right and was shocked by my strong reaction. He himself was not superstitious, and I know he did not believe that I did what I declared. But knowing my loving character and tendencies for tricks, he got the message.

# CHAPTER VI.

## MOVING TO PHAN THIẾT

After finishing my sixth grade, my father was promoted again. This time he would supervise a province named Phan Thiết. The political climate remained turbulent. We had the Vietnamese government, the French, the Japanese, and the Việt Minh militants who were becoming stronger every day.

At first, we stayed in a school close to town. My youngest sister, Phùng Thăng (meaning coincide with a promotion) was about a year old. A young maid named Con Thơm, about 10 years old, was living with us. Con Thơm was my playmate and my special servant. We had a good time chasing after the chameleons in the school yard before they disappeared into their holes. These colorful lizards were sold by the dozen at the market. There were large escargots in Phan Thiết. Some were bigger than a chicken egg. Here was the first time I heard a talking lizard named cackay because he went "cackay cackay" very loud. Cackay was the first word that my baby sister learned to imitate.

I used to take my Phùng Thăng to a corner of the school building to hide when there was a military siren. The English American allies aircraft would bomb and shoot at the Japanese residences. One of these was located next to the school where we lived. I saw a few Japanese officers who did not hide from the air raid. Instead, they went out under a big tree and tried to shoot at the aircraft. My parents were very scared and moved the family to a house inside the Province Chief's compound, far away from town. My uncle, Ưng An, was the Vice Chief at the time. My friend, Xuantu's father, was the Province Chief. Somehow, the Japanese officers occupied a big house in the compound. A Vietnamese Sergeant's family also lived behind our house.

Two Japanese officers came to communicate in writing with my father. They wrote in Chinese characters and seemed to understand each other. One officer tried to teach me and Con Thơm Japanese. We did not bother to learn but we loved to visit them, watching their beautiful tall horses and their short soldiers. Sometimes they gave us cookies or candies. The soldiers were very polite and disciplined. When a soldier wanted to talk to an officer, he did a triple greeting. He would bow at the entrance, then bow again midway, then again in front of the officer before he spoke or listened to an order. I thought the Japanese were nice at that time, they were courageous, polite, and well disciplined. I did not learn about their cruelty to the Vietnamese people until much later. They used to give me and Con Thơm a ride to and from the market in their jeep. And they always treated us with respect.

I noticed that everywhere in Phan Thiết people were growing cotton. They also grew cotton in our garden where once I saw two large snakes twisting around each other and standing vertical like a twisted stick. This sight stopped me from roaming around the garden to search for crickets and grasshoppers.

The Vietnamese sergeant's daughters were also my friends. I watched them spinning yarn out of I cotton long puffs from a simple machine operated by hand. I tried to spin and it was easy. I convinced my mother to buy me a machine. We went into town to get the cotton puffs worked them into yarn. We returned the yarn and got paid by the kilogram. I asked my mother why people did not grow rice as usual. She said the Japanese foster the growing of cotton to get cotton seed oil for their machinery.

One morning, I saw people walking around excited, tense and whispering to each other. A short time later, two Vietnamese strangers came to our house. My father was reading at his desk. One man said, "There was a coup this morning." My father asked, "What do you mean by a coup?" He replied in an arrogant voice explaining the coup while turning his hand in a prone and supine position many times. They told my father that the Việt Minh took control, and the old regime was being replaced.

My mother was very indignant. We were used to polite and courteous treatment. This insolence was new to us. But my mother did know that if they handcuffed my father and took him away, we could not do anything about it! Unless my father had some students or relatives who were high ranked in the new regime! Thank God that my father was always naive, honest, and friendly toward others. He did not use his position to oppress his subordinates. He made no enemies during his career.

After the coup, my parents decided to return home to Vỹ Dạ. We took the train north to Huế. My uncle Ưng Du asked my parents to supervise his four teenaged children to ensure a safe trip home. The train was very crowded. We had to stand up or take turns sitting. There was no room to lie down. The train stopped at a station after twelve hours ride and we slept over at a relative's house to take the train again in the morning. I was so tired that I felt very happy to be able to lie down and stretch my arms and legs. This experience reminded me that it is a blessing to lie down every day in a peaceful quiet room.

# BACK TO VỸ DẠ FOR THE SECOND TIME

After the coup, my father took an early retirement. Middle class people like us became poor after a short time, due to unemployment. Lower class people were not better off.

Many families died from starvation especially the boat people. I discovered for the first time that people spent about thirty percent of their daily expenses on firewood, and seventy percent on rice and other food. Rice was the main dish of the family. We needed only rice and steamed potato leaf dipped in a shrimp sauce to survive. We had a large garden with many jack fruit trees, bamboo shoots, bananas, and starfruit trees. We also grew vegetables and had plenty of food. We did not have to worry about firewood because we could use dead and dry branches and leaves to put in the stove. The boat people had nothing but fish. Sometimes they traded a small basket full of fish and shrimps for only a pound of rice. They could not survive on fish only. They needed real firewood, not dead leaves, and rice to make soup.

Someday, on my way to school, I saw one or two cachectic bodies place on the side of the causeway across the river. A hat was placed close by to receive charity from pedestrians. Those corpses were from the boat people, starved to death. I connected the tragedy with the Japanese people making our farmers grow cotton for them instead of rice for our people. There were rumors that the Japanese used paddies to feed the train engine, instead of coals, to cause starvation. I began to hate the inhuman acts of the Japanese.

Every day, on my way to Đồng Khánh Junior High School, I had to walk past one block occupied by the Japanese. before, this block had been occupied by the French and they did not bother us. Now the Japanese soldiers carried their guns pointing at us when we passed by and made us walk on the other side of the street. There was a rumor that the Japanese would punish a thief by cutting off his index finger. Everyone was afraid of the Japanese because of their cruelty! I realized that the Japanese were much worse than the

French in spite of their propaganda that they would help us because we were from the same continent (Asia), race, religion (Buddhist), and culture!

After they made the French their prisoners overnight without a struggle, we felt sorry for the French who had been our invaders for one hundred years! Tears came to my eyes when I saw the arrogant and aggressive Japanese soldiers escorting the French prisoners who looked helpless with downcast eyes.

## BAD NEWS FROM THE JUNGLE

It was toward the end of World War II. the political situation in Việt Nam was still very confused. My uncle by marriage TT Dat, who was the Minister of Education had just lost his position, together with five other ministers. The Japanese were roaming the street of the old capital Huế. The French officers were still there.

My brother Bửu Đà was about 22 years old and had finished school. He had joined some new mysterious group. He said he went to the mountains to cut trees to sell wood. One day, he gave my mother his ring and some money saying, "Mama, keep these for your expense. If in three weeks you do not hear from me, don't wait for me any longer."

My mother exclaimed, "Why do you talk so strangely? You always told me when you would come back, and you always kept your promise! What is different this time?" My brother remained silent for a while and then said, "Mama, you don't need to know. I don't want to answer too many questions." My mother understood after a long sigh.

Since that day, my mother looked anxious and worried. Just like my oldest brother Minh, brother Đà used to offer my mother part of his salary to raise the family. He was my mother's favorite. She used to cook for him special dishes and he would give us half of his goodies. I would share with my brother Đích who was brother Da's "enemy". When I questioned my mother about her favoritism, she said, "I felt sorry for him because he worked in the mountains and jungles. He rarely came home; therefore, he deserved special treatment!" I also felt sad because my mother was tense and unhappy.

One day, I woke up after midnight and came to my mother's bedside. I was sobbing uncontrollably. My mother tenderly held me in her arms, saying, "Poor child, why are you so sad? You usually don't cry easily." I explained, "I had a bad dream, and I woke up afraid that you might die and leave me an orphan!" My mother consoled me, "Don't say sad things! I am strong and will live to see you grow up! Now go back to sleep."

A few days later, people from the south brought back the news that my brother Bửu Đà was killed in a battle against the enemies. They organized a big ceremony in our family pagoda, to give him the title "The People's Hero" and "The Nation Acknowledges Your Work" award.

After the ceremony, mother asked a relative to go south to look for my brother's grave. Reportedly the local people showed where my brother was buried but we are not sure because there was no tombstone. Our family was very sad after this loss because my brother Bửu Đà was the best man in the family, being very smart, popular, and liberal.

## THE FRENCH RETURNED TO POWER, AIDED BY THE ALLIES

When I was studying the first semester of seventh grade, the Allies defeated the Japanese, the Germans, and Italians, and ended World War II. At the same time, the French were returned to Việt Nam.

The schools were closed because the Việt Minh gave orders to retreat to the jungles. People moved to the countries believing that the French would invade Huế. Our family moved to a small village far away from Huế to avoid the French invasion. Ironically, the invasion began from the countryside not very far away from the sea. We watched the French army marching toward Huế.

They did not shoot, rob, or rape as we expected. Some of them asked to buy eggs. When our land lady learned of the request, she collected about a dozen of eggs and ran after the French soldiers to donate her eggs out of gratitude because they were not violently disturbing the villagers. She was very imprudent because if the Việt Minh knew about this, her family would be in big trouble.

My mother sent me and my two younger sisters to An Nong, to live with my sister-in-law's family. They were among the rich people in the village, but the Việt Minh somehow left them alone and did not bother them. My big brother Minh bought some land in the mountain and grew cassava and sweet potatoes. He hired a young farmer named Hai to take care of his crop. His farm was close to his wife's family home where we lived. My brother Đích joined Hai to work on the farm. Đích was very excited about his new job and composed poems and songs to celebrate his "new life." He told me funny stories about farming.

One day, I visited the farm. We went to the pond to get fish and shrimp for dinner. They placed the bait in basket with lid which had the form of a funnel. When the fish swam in, it was hard to escape, and they often never got out. Hai submerged the basket in the pond for one or two days to catch the fish. When Hai pulled up the basket, it was fairly heavy. He was very happy, laughing and cheering, "Wow, we must have caught a lot of fish!" When he opened the basket, he looked disappointed and surprised. He cursed, "Damned! it's a turtle!" I could not understand because I thought we were luckier to get a turtle because we could play with it!

I asked Đích why Hai swore when he saw the turtle. Đích explained, "Because the turtle ate all our fish!" Đích told me the following story: Hai raised two dogs in the farm to keep him company when we were not there. The dogs also helped him chase the wild swine who came dig up and ate his cassava roots. Hai proudly named the dogs Com and Bat explaining that "We have Combat to fight against our enemies!" Although we are farming to stay away from the war, we are still in the mood! It was very "A la mode" to name the dogs Com Bat in war time. Đích did not know who were Hai's real enemies, was it the Việt Minh? the Japanese? the French? the Allies? or the swine?

One day, when Đích came back from town, Hai prepared a big meal with many dishes of meat, which had become a rarity in those times. Normally, the dogs would run around the table to get their share. Đích only saw one dog running around. He asked, "Where is Bat?" Hai said, "He was already butchered! I sacrificed his dog life for our cause." Đích looked at the dishes on the table. He shook his head but did not ask. He only said, "I am full. I will eat later. You eat first and don't save any for me. I only need rice and fish sauce."

A few months later, Đích left the farm to return to town because ha almost died from pernicious malaria. He said he had many days of alternating chills and fevers, and his urine was dark like black tea due to the destroyed blood.

While we were preparing to return to town because the French and Việt Minh were not fighting, a terrible event precipitated our return. One morning, three bombers passed our village. They went out to the sea and we only saw one flying back. Someone asked, "Why there is only one back?" My sister-in-law's mother said convincingly, "Two of them were shot down to the sea." Other people inquired, very interested to find out the truth, "Where did you get the news? Who said so?" I said, "the old lady reported," and everybody was silent.

The next afternoon, we heard the bombers coming again. Then a few minutes later, we heard machine guns shooting. When the Allies airplanes left, people from my cousin Lin's home came and reported that she was killed by the air raid. Lin was my aunt's daughter. She was married to my sister-in-law's cousin. Lin had two beautiful daughters named Pineapple and Rosa. They said that Lin was in the house when the flames passed by. When the planes were gone, Lin went out to get the red shirt in, saying that it might be mistaken for a Việt Minh Flag. The shirt was hung out that day in the sun. When Lin reached for the shirt and held it in her arm, the airplane made a "U" turn and shot her with machine guns. She died on the spot.

After this accident, we returned home by boat during the night. Another cousin Mụ Chanh, about 25 years old, went with us. She had an infant boy who was very small due to malnutrition. When the boat reached its destination, we had to walk across a few paddy fields before getting home.

We used a storm lamp to guide us in the dark. I carried my youngest sister Phùng Thăng, who was about one and a half years old. I imagined that we might step on some cadaver killed by the Việt Minh or the Allies. They said that some strangers just got killed and nobody buried them. They were left on the spot or pulled to the rice field so that some particular bullhead fish might feed on them. I thought out loud this morbid story and Mụ Chanh was very scared. My sister Phùng Khánh helped carry her baby's stuff.

When we reached home, Mụ Chanh came directly to my mother and said, "Have pity on me, dear aunt, my baby and I had never been so miserable!" My mother said, "Don't cry, don't lament, you are safe and sound. Let me hold the baby. Where is he?" Mụ Chanh showed my mother an empty towel where she had wrapped her baby earlier. She cried out, "Oh, God, I dropped him enroute!"

My mother told everybody to look for the baby and luckily, we found him not too far away and brought him back. Mụ Chanh complained incessantly about me "Cousin Phùng Mai did not help us at all. She only spent time scaring me! Phùng Khánh is a buddha herself. She helped me a lot. I will place her on an altar to worship her!" I said, "But thanks to my jokes that the trip was short and fun! I expected the worse and we were happy that we did not get it!" My mother told me not to tease her anymore, but I thought Mụ Chanh was kind of dramatic and ridiculous!

## MY MOTHER TREATED MARASMUS

When Mụ Chanh showed my mother her three months old baby boy, we all felt very sorry for him. He was so malnourished that he was only skin and bone. He was a tall baby, but he held his arms and legs in flexion that reduced his length by half. Besides, his caseous bone stuck out like a real tail bone. I thought he was in a fetal position because he was cold, but it was not the case. When we brought him close to the fireplace to keep him warm, he still would not straighten his limbs. Mụ Chanh tried to pull his arms and legs straight, but she couldn't because of the contracted tendons of his joints. He would moan in a weak soft voice when his mother tried to correct his body position. My mother sighed, "Poor little boy. Your mother does not know how to care for a baby."

"But thank Buddha, it is not too late!" Mụ Chanh was crying like this was the first time that she discovered her baby's sickness. My mother consoled her and assured that she will help her caring for her child.

Then my mother started her "healing art". She told a servant to boil water and poured it into a basin. She put a few teaspoons of sea salt in it. When the water was lukewarm, she placed the infant in the basin, holding his head up, while talking to him. She told Mụ Chanh and me to wash our hands then try to massage the baby's knees and elbows in the warm salty water.

The baby looked comfortable and happy. His joints were less stiff, and we could slowly straighten them up. After about fifteen to twenty minutes, we rinsed him with warm water and dried him up. He was softer and more flexible. We bathed him daily. After a few days, he was able to extend his limbs freely. My mother fed him with brown rice soup as a vitamin supplement. She fed his mother with chicken eggs and meat to enrich her milk for breast feeding. After a few months, the baby gained weight, looked stronger, and happier. Mụ Chanh was ready to take him to the jungle in search of his father. Afterward, we heard that the family reunified and were healthy and safe.

# CHAPTER VII.

## BACK TO VỸ DẠ THE SECOND TIME

After the retreat of the Việt Minh, a new government was formed headed by the former Emperor Bảo Đại[6], who was now titled the Chief of State. Việt Nam was divided into three regions: North, South, and Central headed by a Vietnamese governor. But because the French still had their military and cultural influence, the Việt Minh called this a puppet government and they continued to fight with the French. This headed in a climax in the battle of Điện Biên Phủ in 1954.

The Việt Minh still controlled the distant villages and infiltrated villages and districts to assassinate their chiefs. They buried mines at night and blew up French vehicles as they passed by the next day.

At the time, my sister-in-law Chị Hoa's nephew, Hà was living with us. One day, a French jeep was detonated close to our home. During their subsequent search of the area surrounding the destruction, the French discovered Hà in our house calmly studying.

---

[6] Élysée Accords on 9 March 1949

They arrested and incarcerated him, suspecting his involvement. His family asked my father to get him out of jail. My father talked to his French friends and teachers asking them to intervene. Hà was released and returned to his village An Nông[7].

Months later, while we slept, dogs in the neighborhood suddenly started barking. We knew that the Việt Minh were roaming the neighborhood. The sounds of gunshots made us fear for our safety. Minutes later, our tension was broken by the sound of somebody knocking at the window.

It was a familiar voice, "Madam, don't be afraid, this is Hà!"

We were more frightened by the suspicious calmness of his reassurance. My mother said, "Amita Buddha, Hà. Keep going and taking care of yourself!"

This encounter unsettled me and was the moment I doubted his innocence.

The Việt Minh made excellent propaganda. They wrote beautiful songs and poems to spread their message. I can still recall:

*Together with the forest and mountains, we fight the French.*
*The mountains spread into a high wall becoming a thick fortress.*
*The forest protects our army and surrounds our enemies.*

This continued…

*Using the mountains and forest to conquer the villages.*
*Using the villages to seize the towns and cities.*

And it was with this strategy, they defeated the French at Điện Biên Phủ

---

[7] For more details refer to *Exhibit B* at the end of the book

# CHAPTER VIII.

## MY IDLE TIME

During this transition, most people were unemployed and poor. Our family had no income, so my mother took advantage of our river dock to buy fish and sell fish sauce and firewood. She would buy a boat full of firewood to sell to our neighbors. One bundle of firewood might double or triple its price after six months. We used to buy them in spring and summer and sell them in winter. She bought many large containers of shrimp paste and sold them by the ounce. With this business, my mother made enough money to feed the family even if we had to ration rice and food.

### CON THƠM

I still got to keep my favorite servant and friend, Con Thơm. One day, her father came and said in an arrogant voice, "Now, there are no more mistresses or servants. Everybody is equal and free. Thơm, go home with daddy. I am taking you home." Con Thơm replied, no less arrogant, "No, I am not going home. I am staying with sister Phùng Mai. Now that I am independent and free, I can choose whatever I want. I decide to stay! Daddy, you go home without me!"

I applauded Con Thơm, "Bravo, Thơm, you are very advanced and revolutionary. Very fashionable! You deserve to be my disciple!" Con Thơm was very happy living with us. Everywhere I went, she was by my side. I would teach her the meanings of new revolutionary words such as independence, freedom, revolution, etc... which were "inflated" at that time. I would tell her jokes and she would laugh happily. She would do anything for me to make her laugh.

In our back garden, there lived some family who kept our garden in good shape. They had a disabled pre-adolescent boy who had encephalitis and severe cerebral palsy. One day he swore at me and Con Thơm because he thought we were pulling up his turnips.

I just repeated the phrase "Pulling up turnips, pulling up turnips" and he would swear and call his grandpa to tell. He talked in such a funny way that I enjoyed making him repeat. And each time he swore at me, Con Thơm would have a hearty laugh. Later, I used to play double roles, repeating my teasing and his swearing to entertain Con Thơm. She would give me her rice and food to make her laugh.

Com Thơm even let me cut her hair. She was a very beautiful girl with dark hair, dove eyes, light skin, and red lips. I took the occasion to talk her into letting me shave her head to look like a young Buddhist nun. I shaved her hair everywhere except three places-one part in front, and one part on each side. She was about ten years old and looked so cute with her new haircut. Everybody praised her about her hair and face, and she looked like a real nun.

Unfortunately, one day we happened to discover something very troubling about Con Thơm. My brother, Địch, and I were eating jackfruit while sitting on the branches of the jackfruit tree. Suddenly, we saw Con Thơm running after a group of newly hatched yellow chickens. The protest of the mother hen drew our attention to Con Thơm because she was proceeding in a very cautiously.

We saw her catch two baby chickens then dig a hole to bury them. All this happened so fast that we did not have time to stop her, we were still processing what we saw.

When we yelled out "Thom, what are you doing?" She was surprised and startled "They are dead!" We climbed down the tree and she asked, "Since when were you up there? I did not see you. If I had seen you, I would have joined you, I would not bother the chickens!"

I asked her why she did it, and she said, "Because they are so beautiful, I had to kill them!" I explained to her the Buddhist first law "Not to kill" and how cruel it is to kill those beautiful creatures. She promised me that she would never do it again. "No matter how beautiful they are!" I reminded her "Don't you know that you are beautiful yourself."

"You don't want anybody to kill you because you are pretty, do you?" To this day I could not understand why she did what she did. Maybe out of jealousy?

Getting bored playing around, I wanted to go back to school, and told my mother. Surprisingly, she said, "We have no money to send you to school." I replied "I still eat two meals a day whether I go to school or not. What is the extra cost?" She answered, "Clothing and books!" and I agreed to stay home. It was my big sister, Khánh Trợ, who sent me back to school after she returned from her exodus.

I could not stay inactive and decided to buy and sell rice. My mother gave me one hundred piasters to start. I went with Con Thơm to buy two baskets and the equipment to carry them at the end of a long stick which is placed on your shoulder. We also bought a small chair to sit on the ground in the market. The next morning, we woke up early and went to a market in the countryside, about five miles from our house. Con Thơm was very excited about my new project. The equipment cost about twenty piasters. We got eighty piasters for the rice. After selling the rice, we were supposed to get at least twenty piasters profit. With this profit, we could buy grocery or rice to feed the family for one day.

I did all the calculations while Con Thom would do all the labor including measuring the rice and carrying it. We went to the largest market in town to sell the rice. Each customer would buy four or five units (about 1 1/2 cup) and we got about 200 units to sell.

Beyond my expectation, many ragged, starved skinny beggars passed by and asked for charity; I could not resist and started giving them by handfuls into their small wooden bowls. Con Thom was busy measuring the rice for the customers. Sometimes she yelled out "Sister, you've already gave this woman twice, don't you remember?" How could I remember because they all looked the same with their skinny bodies, torn clothing, and pitiful faces.

We sold our merchandise very fast. But when we counted the money, we only got eighty piasters, short of twenty bucks, because I had given away my profit. Con Thom was frustrated "Sister, I had wasted my labor to carry those heavy baskets, but we did not get any profit out of it." And I reminded her, "But didn't we have lots of fun? I asked to help carrying them, but you wouldn't let me!" And she laughed. I promised her to make her happy, "I will let you tell Madam the story about why we did not make any profit, OK?" And she was content. When she told my mother about our adventure, at first, my mother asked me "Where is the profit?" I told her" The equipment is the profit!" My mother knew better. "NO, you used part of the capital to buy the equipment!"

I answered, "I used all the profit to buy happiness for the poor people!" My mother smiled forgivingly "See, I knew that you could not do this. You are too soft- hearted!"

Con Thom asked me to think about another project so that we could work together. I asked her what she could do. She said, "I can go selling things by myself without you! You wait at home, and I'll bring back the money that I'll make for you." I thought about selling

MY IDLE TIME

steamed sweet pastry because we were low on rice but had plenty of mung beans, cassava powder, and sugar in the market. We had plenty of banana leaves for the wrapping. I took Con Thơm out to buy fifty piasters worth of the ingredients. I made the dough, prepared the sweet mung bean, and divided the dough into two hundred parts and the mung bean paste into two hundred balls. Then I asked my two sisters to join me and Con Thơm rolling the dough around the center balls and wrapping them up.

I ensured that I would double my capital to one hundred piasters by selling two pastries for piaster. Con Thơm was very happy to cook the pastries and keep them warm in a basket. She went out selling them door to door. She would tell the buyers, "These were made by my sister Phùng Mai. Please try them. They are very good and tasty." Most of the buyers were our relatives, and they knew me. After two or three hours, she would return with about ninety-five to one hundred piasters. The missing cash was due to some people who did not have enough cash that day and promised to pay the next day. I would give Con Thơm fifty piasters to go buy the ingredients and prepare the pastries for the following day.

Our sweets were good and relatively cheap and would be sold out very fast once Con Thơm knew her customers. It was cheap because I did not count the cost of banana leaves and firewood to add into the capital. I gave Con Thơm some allowance for her good work, but what made her most happy was that she could make money to buy groceries for the family as I put it. She was very proud of herself, "Sister Phùng Mai, we are doing great, aren't we?" When this news reached my big sister Khánh Trợ, who was in the jungle, she burst into tears thinking that I was the peddler selling food from door to door, despite being so afraid of the dogs!

Con Thơm was very generous and honest. When her mother was sick and she had to go home to care for her, she cried and told me, "I will miss you every day. I will return when my mother feels better. Here are forty-five piasters that the customers owed you. You don't know them and cannot collect from them. I want you to keep your money now, and I will collect it later!" How noble she was! Naturally my mother gave her some money before she went home to care for her sick mother.

When Con Thơm came back, we had a bad flood. The water rose from the river and our floor was under water by about fifteen inches. We had to wad in muddy water going from room to room for two days, before the water retreated. Con Thơm would be happy to carry me on her back, back and forth from my desk to the dining table, stating, "You don't need to wet your feet, sister. I'm strong enough to be your horse!"

Since we had the flood, we had a good time catching fish with a large net. My big brother fixed for me a net with a pole and cord. We dipped the net in the muddy water for about ten to fifteen minutes then pulled it up and we caught the fish entrapped inside. Con Thơm was eager to catch the fish with her hands and put them in a large bucket. We used to fish at night because that was the time that the fish did not see the net and would get into the trap. I was cautious and told Con Thơm to bring the lantern over to see before she picked up the fish.

Close to midnight, we made a half bucket of fish and we were very excited. Once we pulled up a large snake about sixty inches long which had curled up on the bottom of the net. We could not tell where its head or tail were because both ends of the snake looked the same. I told Con Thơm, "See, you always have to look under the light before you pick up something moving!"

She said, "If I did not listen to you, I would have been bitten by the snake!" We did not want any fish in that net occupied by the snake. We dipped it down and waited for the snake to leave. After a moment, we pulled up the net and the snake was still there! I told Con Thơm "Now it's time for us to stop fishing. We had enough fish. Don't you think so?" She agreed" Yes, let's go and show the bucket to the family!"

It was almost midnight and everybody was still waiting for us. We mentioned about the snake, and my mother said, "Only he can stop you from committing the sin of fishing!" and I reminded her "But you love to eat fish, mama!"

One evening, I heard somebody moaning painfully by the edge of the river. I ran down. It was Con Thơm who sat on the ground with both hands holding her left foot. Her body and face were twisted with pain. She said, "I believe I was bitten by a toad!" I felt so sorry for her and took her to the hospital to get her wound cleaned and to get her a tetanus shot. She was given some pain pills and sent home. I had never seen anybody who was in so much pain! She was in pain for three days despite the medicine.

Con Thơm went back to her house when she was about fifteen or sixteen years old, preparing to get married. A few years later, I learned that she was married. One evening, she came to visit us, very distraught. I could not understand how a happy pleasant girl with bright eyes, and ever smiling face could turn into a sad, fearful, hopeless woman in a short time! I asked her what had happened· and she told me her story.

Her parents wanted her to marry a man who was a police officer. The man lived with his mother and a twenty-year-old brother and had many male and female friends who visited them almost every day. Con Thơm's mother-in-law bought the equipment for her to sell soybean yogurt door to door. She was ordered to finish early and bring home seventy piasters every day. When the weather changed and the yogurt spoiled, she had to use her own money to make up for the loss.

This would happen often. Con Thơm had used up her savings and would come home short of ten or twenty piasters. Her mother-in-law and brother-in-law would yell at her, beat her up, and take away her dinner. When her husband came home, they would accuse her of giving away the money to her boyfriend, gambling it away, or using it for snacks. Then, she would receive another beating. Sometimes her husband's friends would join in the physical and verbal abuse. As she told me her story, I was imagining a pack of hunting dogs surrounding their prey! Con Thơm was sobbing while telling me her story, "They really hate me. They abuse me every day, I cannot go on like this." I asked her why she didn't get a divorce and return to live with her parents or us. She said her husband promised to kill her or put her in jail if she dared to leave his family.

I was infuriated. I talked to my sister Khánh Trợ who decided to adopt Con Thơm and send her to live with my big brother in Đà Lạt. Đà Lạt was the "Royal Land" at that time, people had to have the government's permission to move to Đà Lạt. Since my big brother belonged to the royal family, Con Thơm's husband had a very slim chance of finding out that she moved there and the minimal chance of reaching her. We told Con Thơm to start her day as she usually did. Around noon, she would leave her merchandise and equipment at the market, get her ticket, and fly to Đà Lạt. My brother would meet her there and add her to his large family. She started to call me Auntie Phùng Mai like my brother's children from then on.

## WE ADOPTED AN ORPHAN GIRL

One summer day, my sister and I went to the market. We saw a nine or ten-year-old girl sobbing in the middle of a small crowd. Her parents were deceased and she was just abandoned by her uncle who was too poor to feed her. She did not know how to start a beggar's life.

Seeing me, some woman in the crowd said, "Miss Phùng Mai, why don't you take her home and save her life. She has nobody to turn to." My sister Phùng Khánh, who later became a Buddhist nun, added, "Lets, do it, sister."

I asked the little girl, "Do you want to come home to live with my family?" She said, "yes," and brightened up a little bit. I said, "Then, dry up your tears and come home with us." and we took her home. On our way home, while navigating the boat, my sister Phùng Khánh began to plan, "We will feed her, clean her up, cut her hair, and dress her up. We will call her Con Lan, OK sister?" I agreed, and the poor girl had a new name "Lan" meaning orchid.

When we got home, I was proud to display to my mother our new discovery, "Mama, look what we found in the market! Phùng Khánh already gave her a name "Orchid!" We told my mother the story, and she sadly said, "Poor child! She must be starving! Let's feed her first then you will clean her up next!"

After Con Lan ate, we started combing her hair. Her hair was so entangled that it looked like a woven hat on her head with many long strings sticking out here and there like a bird's nest. Under the nest, large black head lice were running in different directions. We could not clearly see the lice but there must be thousands of them. There was no place to get the comb in the nest. I decided, "There is no need to comb and no way to save her hair which is so infested with lice. We can just cut it close to the scalp then give her a thorough shampoo to get rid of the remaining lice." So we did that and burned the cut hair for infection control. We took her to our river, cleaned her with soap and gave her new clothing to put on.

She became a different person, a pretty girl with a light complexion, possible due to anemia, and large dark brown eyes. With our tender loving care, she flourished, gained weight, and even had some color in her cheeks. She became cheerful, active, and helpful. She would ask to help with any chore in the home that she could, such as growing vegetables, sweeping the floor, washing the dishes, etc... She was eager to learn to work and to everybody she would offer herself to do odd jobs.

When her thick black hair grew back, she looked like a pretty Japanese doll with her large eyes. We taught her to read and write and she was very intelligent and learned fast. We were very pleased with her progress; she looked like an Orchid unfolding its petals daily in front of our eyes! She was my sister Phùng Khánh's playmate because she was much younger than I. She was very thankful to me for having brought her home. She used to offer me her help, "Sister Phùng Mai, what can I help you today?" I would give her a choice "Work in the kitchen, in the garden or do things for me?" Orchid always chose to work for me.

One winter morning, I woke up late and did not see Orchid around. I asked Phùng Khánh where she was. Phùng Khánh said she was still in bed, sick. I found that Orchid was very tired with a fever. We took her to the hospital and visited her every day. One afternoon, when we came to visit, we were told that Orchid had died that morning, and was sent to the morgue. With broken hearts, we went directly to the morgue, a place that we always hated when we passed by. Our Orchid was there, lying peacefully in a bed like she was asleep, waiting to be buried.

We hurried home to tell our mother. My mother asked our cousin Chị Vân to escort Orchid to her grave. My sister Phùng Khánh and I went with Chị Vân to escort Orchid to her last peaceful rest. When we reached the morgue, Orchid was already placed in a coffin provided by the hospital. Two hospital laborers carried her coffin to the mountains nearby to bury her. We cried silently.

Chị Vân said, "Don't cry. Do you want the men to drop the coffin on the road for you to carry it? Orchid supposedly has no relatives, that's why the hospital took care of the funeral and burial." One man who carried the coffin asked "Where are you from? "Before we could answer him, Chị Vân said, "Gia Hai!" I thought she made a mistake and was about to correct her. She said in a low voice, "Quiet. Is there anything glamorous about death and funeral to mention our real village's name, Vỹ Dạ? When there is something negative to say, just mention another village!" She said this in such a funny manner that I wanted to laugh but I looked over at my sister Phùng Khánh and saw that she was not in a mood for laughing. Thinking about our love and respect toward Orchid, I refrained myself from laughing.

Chị Vân was a single woman about fifty-five years old at the time. Our family loved and respected her for her intelligence and helpfulness. When her family was living in Phan Thiết and her mother died, she was able to transport her mother home to be buried in the family cemetery in Huế. It was a very piteous and courageous action because she had to deal with the French and Vietnamese officials to transport a dead person by train. She had to meet all the requirements of public health and hygiene and provide an odor-proof tin coffin for inspection, etc... before she could get the permit to transport.

## SELLING INDOCHINA CURRENCY

After Orchid's death, I looked for some new activity. My friend and cousin, Pearl, was selling currencies at that time, and I decided to join her in the venture. When the French returned to Việt Nam, people were using both Indochina and Việt Minh's currencies at the same ratio of one to one. Some businessmen wanted to pay one and a half of Việt Minh's piasters for one Indochina piaster. Pearl and I went to the bicycle taxi drivers and peddlers to buy Indochina currency at a lower price then resell them. I did not care much about making money this way. All that interested me was going places with Pearl and listening to her stories and jokes. Pearl had a way of turning daily life events into hilarious stories.

One day, we went past a private school name Viet Huong, meaning the fragrance of Việt Nam. It was an all-girl secondary school. It was recess time and we saw the students playing in the school yard. Pearl told me, "Let's stop here to see what kind of tricks these female goblins are doing." We stopped by the gate and looked in. A few old friends saw us and ran out to talk to us. One of them was Túy Thiện, a very nice, noble, and shy girl that we could easily bully but wouldn't. Túy Thiện talked about who were back in school, who were not, who were the teachers, etc... She asked us to go back to school, "It is fun!" We said, "Maybe, we will think about it." After this conversation, something sank in my heart. I came to terms with reality telling myself, "I've been fooling around long enough. If I don't return to school, I will be behind all these friends forever!"

## CHAPTER IX.

### BACK TO SCHOOL

When my sister Khánh Trợ came back from the jungle, she helped me to turn in an application for the eighth-grade entry exam. I only had one or two months of seventh grade before the school was closed due to the war, but I read through a few seventh-grade books and passed the exam. I was placed in the same class as Túy Thiện and Pearl.

I still fooled around after I returned to school. My extracurricular activities were raising ducks and buying groceries on my way back from school. Every day, I would stop by the market and buy vegetables, meat, clams, etc... My friends would offer to carry the stuff for me when I had too many packages. Pearl and I made a team to share our joke about the other five or six girls who used to take the same boat to cross the river.

My other cousin in the same class was named DT, who also had a nickname meaning "girl." She had a very close friend whose name also meant "boy" which we always used to tease them about. Later, after they had a falling out, I became fairly close to Boy after Pearl moved away. At that time, Pearl's family moved to Sài Gòn, the current capital of Việt Nam, when her older brother took the position of Prime Minister.

We had about twenty-five girls in our class. We were the most playful class in the entire school. Our teachers always noticed how close knit we were. I was lazy and never brought lunch for myself. I believed that I could skip lunch because I was strong, muscular, and heavy enough. But my classmates always shared their meal with me during lunch time.

Recently I met Đăng Nga and Pearl who just came to America in 1993. Đăng Nga reminded us of our old times when he recounted, "We competed to get Phùng Mai to eat lunch with us!" We used lunch time to read novels, poems, and sing together in small groups. Sometimes we gathered to listen to Pearl stories. Some of our classmates used to come to my house to learn how to swim. We would cut a banana trunk to serve as a floater.

Recently one of my former classmates, Liên Hải, reminisced during a class reunion, "Phùng Mai, do you remember once, I almost drowned and called for help. And you said, 'Wait, let me get some foxtail aqua for the ducks first!'" I did not forget and reminded her "But I did tow you with my banana trunk, didn't I?"

One day, somebody, maybe Liên Hải, had the idea to go to the river across the street from our school. This was forbidden by the school superintendent. This one used to scold us ironically "You are so virtuous that you would stomp on your mother-in-law to break her urinary bladder!" About eight or ten of us took the challenge. We climbed over the school wall to get on the street because the gate was locked. When we were playing with the water in the river, the superintendent materialized like an apparition! Everybody turned their back and ran back to school so that they could not be recognized. I thought to myself, "If we run in a hurry, we may fall or get hit by a car. It's better to admit to our mistake and the punishment."

And so, I remained on the spot. The superintendent was very nice to me and she was happy because she could catch at least one witness! She told me that I was honest and asked me the names of the girls who had broken the school rules. I gave the names. She came to our class, lectured us about girl's good manners, and named her punishment: we had to stay back an hour after school was over. The rest of our classmates volunteered to stay with us after school so that we could have an extra fun time together.

I felt like a traitor after having told on my friends. But nobody called me that name or confronted me with my cowardice. They just accepted me as I was. I loved them dearly for their mercy and support.

Once, I noticed a small group discussing the book "Uncle Tom's Cabin." I wanted to borrow the book from them to read. My cousin DT said, "Phùng Mai, you might not understand this book. It's too hard for you. Go home and finish your sixth-grade reading book first!"

It was a heavy blow to my pride. I promised to myself to excel in all five major subjects: English, French, Vietnamese, Math, and Sciences. Starting from that day, I learned by heart one lesson each day in that sixth-grade book. Every morning, I asked my sister-in-law, Hoa, to follow my memorized lesson by reading the book. I worked my way into becoming the class valedictorian.

## THE EXCHANGE OF THE VALEDICTORIAN SPEECH

During my last year in junior high school, there were meetings to protest the French government in Sài Gòn. One student was killed by the police. The Dean of our school told me to write a speech in commemoration of the deceased fellow student. Knowing that I was a peaceful industrious student, far away from being involved in politics, she had confidence in me. I prepared the speech and let her review it first. She highly approved of the speech and recommended me to read it in front of the crowd.

When I was standing on the podium ready to deliver my speech, my friend Liên Hải came by and whispered, "Phùng Mai, you take a seat and rest. Let me read it for you!" I was so naive and trustful that I agreed to let her read my speech.

I thought she would have a good voice because she played a role in our class play. And of course, listening to someone else reading your work could be more fun! I gave Liên Hải my paper and went down to the audience, took a seat, waiting for her to read my composition.

Surprisingly, she put my paper in her pocket and pulled out another one. She began to read this paper full of bloody hatred which aroused anger and vengeance in the audience. I could not do anything about it because the students were so excited.

After the speech, Liên Hải was arrested by the Security Agency. We did go visit her in her confinement. It turned out that another classmate, Boy, gave Liên Hải the speech in exchange for mine. Liên Hải was released due to her family's influence. Her family decided to send her to America to continue her education.

Recently, in 1994, a friend of mine Rosa, stopped by Hà Nội to visit Boy. Rosa asked her about the incident, and Boy said that she knew if Liên Hải was arrested, her family could get her out easily, "Nobody else in our class could have done that job!"

Another surprise for me was that I never got reprimanded by the Dean for my forfeiture. Perhaps she thought I was forced to give up my speech. The political atmosphere of the time had made people more cautious.

## MY LAST YEARS IN HIGH SCHOOL

After junior high, we began to specialize either in math, sciences, or languages. I knew that I could not compete with some students who were very good at math. I chose sciences because I wanted to prepare to study medicine. After a few weeks in sciences, I accumulated many chapters that I was supposed to memorize.

Seeing that there was no fun in doing this kind of hard work, I switched to studying languages. I loved to study French, English, and Vietnamese literature. I tried to be helpful to my classmates by translating difficult words for them. Even in the written exam, I attempted to write large letters and meanings so that my friends sitting behind me could read and copy. An examiner warned me, "Phùng Mai, if you still write large letters like that, I will ask you to leave the classroom." When he saw me outside, he said, "Miss Phùng Mai, why were you so humane?" and I answered "Teacher, because I want all my classmates to pass the test."

I began in a co-ed classroom starting the tenth grade. We stayed in the same room and had the same teachers for each school year. Only the teachers had to move from room to room to teach his or her classes. The number of classmates seemed to drop down yearly. We had about thirty-five to forty students in tenth grade, twenty-five to thirty students in eleventh grade, and only fifteen to sixteen in twelfth grade. Most of the male students dropped out because they were recruited by the military services.

I did very well in my last year in high school. I managed to stay top of my class every month. Thanks to our math teacher, Ha Thuc, I achieved a high average each month. He would give me ten points out of ten when the students wanted me to repeat his teaching on a new lesson. This sometimes raised my point average to eight point five (8.5).

Teacher Hà Thúc was very helpful because it was very hard to get an average of seven out of ten in literature and philosophic dissertations. I ended up receiving an award of excellence for having the highest point average in my class, an honor award for having the most certificates of merit. I also got the Honor Award of the whole school due to my conduct and achievement, and the Bảo Đại Award given to the best student in all high schools (Bảo Đại was the former emperor of Việt Nam and was the Chief of State at that time).

I received the awards for being the best student in five or six different subjects, and with that I got a table full of new books, including dictionaries of many kinds. I also received two grants from the governors of the North and Central regions. I received a scholarship to go to America from Reverend Cao Văn Luận. I asked our high school dean to buy all my books for next year's distribution of awards so that I could have money to buy the ticket to go to America. Two friends of mine, Mỹ Lộc and Diệu Hồi, also received scholarships to go to America. We went together to Sài Gòn to prepare for the departure.

Somehow, both decided to stay in Sài Gòn to study pharmacy. Possibly because Diệu Hồi's brother told her she would be an old spinster after she returned from the U.S. with a university diploma! I called my school in Ohio and asked if they had a pre-med program. They said no and offered me to study education which they felt that Việt Nam needed. However, I wanted to study medicine and decided to stay in Sài Gòn to study pre-med there.

I sent ten thousand piasters home and told my mother to ask my teacher, Doan Tú Thanh, to keep it for me. This was the money I had collected for my travel ticket to the U.S. One year later, I returned to Huế during summer vacation. I visited Reverend Cao Văn Luận. He told me that my friend, Thu Vân, wanted to go to the U.S. and he had no money to help her. I felt a bit guilty for having rejected my scholarship. I told him, "I can let you borrow my money to help Thu Vân to go the U.S."

He was very happy and surprised. I told him that I had asked Mr. Thanh to hold my money for my future education in a foreign country. But I wrote Reverend Luận a note to give to Mr. Thanh to get my ten thousand piasters for Thu Vân's studies in the US.

Years later after my graduation from medical school, I returned to my hometown, Huế, to work in the General Central Hospital. When I saw Reverend Luận, he paid back five thousand and promised to pay the rest later. He never actually did but I did not care since because ten thousand piasters were equivalent to two thousand U.S. dollars when I lent it to him but only eight dollars seven years later when he paid me back.

Twenty-two years later, when I came to the U.S. with my family, I met up with Thu Vân and reminisced about the story of Reverend Luận's scholarship. She was surprised and said she never realized that it was me that helped her during that difficult time!

# CHAPTER X.

## PRE-MED AND MEDICAL SCHOOL

I stayed with Diệu Hồi and her brothers during my pre-med year. In the French program, we had one year of pre-med i.e., PCB (Physics, Chemistry, and Biology) and six years of medicine and clinical training.

I used to ride my bicycle to school, about an hour from home. Two French classmates, Yvette and Francoise, know where I lived and offered to pick me up on their way to school and drop me back driving in Yvette's car. Francoise talked a lot, she used to go to the blackboard to discuss a lesson we had just learned, very sure of herself. Yvette was more humble and cautious. I had the idea that French students could not beat Vietnamese students in their own language.

They were talkative and self-confident but did not do well in written tests. At the end of that year, Yvette dropped by my house and announced, "Phùng Mai, you and I passed the exam. Francoise failed." I did not bother to go look for the results because I knew sooner or later somebody would tell me. My friends used to tease me, "Phùng Mai does not need to take an exam. She already has the diploma in hand!" And I would say "Yes, the professors only need to ask me: Who is your father? How old are you and what is your name? If I answered correctly, they'll let me pass!"

A few months later, Yvette told me that her parents would sell their house and return to Paris. I lost a nice friend and I realized this was an effect of the French boycott by the new regime. Việt Nam was pro-America at that time.

We still had French professors in medical school until I graduated. One day at the end of my first year, I was stopped by a few students at the school gate. One of them said, "Phùng Mai, we don't have class today. We are boycotting the French!" I asked, "Did the professor come?" and the reply was, "Yes, he did." I said, "I don't care. I had used my time and energy to come here. I want to learn or at least say good-bye to my professor. You should have warned me in advance. Now it is too late. If he is in there, I am going to see him!" Surprised by my honesty and stubbornness, they let me go. We had about a dozen of us in class, mostly students from Sài Gòn. They were very respectful and very kind to their teachers. The professor spent half an hour for his lecture and the rest reminiscing about the good old times before saying good-bye.

I lived with my father during the first year of medical school. His house was close to Petrusky College where my father taught for many years. He dedicated to this school a poem in two verses that they wrote on each column of their school gate, "Always remember the moral taught by Confucius. Study hard the sciences and technologies of the Europeans and Americans." Recently I learned from my niece that the new regime was very angry at these recommendations to the students, and they had taken them off from the columns.

One day, there was a battle in town between the government Ngô Đình Diệm and the gang Bình Xuyên. Our house was close to their crossfire. When I heard their gunshots, I remember taking my book and moving to a safe corner to continue reading.

My father said, "Phùng Mai, they are shooting and killing one another out there, aren't you scared? Why are you still studying?"

I replied over the sound of bullets, "We cannot do anything about it! They will stop fighting when one party withdraws. Tomorrow, peace will return. But if I do not study now… I will miss a chapter tomorrow and will be the loser!"

I lived with my brother Đích's family during the second and third years. In his small house, he placed two desks: one for him and one for me. He was so proud, "We look it's as if we were working in an office!" When I was about to leave for America, Đích worried a lot. He said, "I am a man and I am scared to go abroad. You are a young girl, how could you struggle for life in a foreign country?" I said, "I have my sponsor, my brain, and my mouth. What else do I need?" He gave me his whole savings in case I might need it. I sent all my money back to my mother, including his.

I had my fiancé, Đệ, who came and picked me up for school on his Lambretta scooter. One day, while waiting to go in class, Professor Montagne asked me, "How old are you, my little girl?" He used to call me "my little girl." I said, "I am twenty-five years old!" He said, "Twenty-five! You are a big girl. We must think to get you married!" I told him, "I already have a fiancé!" and he said, "Go get your fiancé so that I can meet him." And I brought Đệ to introduce to our professor. We had about one hundred students in our class, and there were less than ten girls in total. The girls used to sit in the front row, so the teachers often knew them better.

I continued to use my "tricks" in college. When I was in the fourth year, a professor named Pequignot, came from Paris to give an oral exam about internal medicine. Everyone feared him. When he was frustrated, his face would turn red, and he would slam his right fist on the table, and he would yell when a student gave him the wrong answer. This happened often enough with many students. Our other

Vietnamese professors, Đệ, and Hữu, watched the scene and looked at each other wondering what made Pequignot so mad.

But when it was my turn, I picked a topic that I knew fairly well. I was not afraid, but I pretended to be frightened. Pequignot was surprised, "Why are you so scared, my little girl?" I replied, "I am scared because neurology is my worst subject; I am afraid that I might displease you." He smiled tolerantly "Come on, don't be afraid, tell me what you know about the subject." And I gave him a thorough and organized report while watching his reaction. His face looked more and more relaxed, and he laughed heartily, "You are doing fine, my little one. See? I am not an ogre to yell at you when you are doing so well!"

I replied, "I believe you. Thank you for not grilling me." And he continued to be in a good mood. When I left his room, I saw Professors Đệ and Hữu standing in the hallway smiling. One of them said, "She succeeded in making Pequignot laugh! She was wonderful!" The other said, "Phùng Mai is terrific!"

When I was in the fourth year of medical school, my sister Phùng Khánh began to study business administration. She stayed in a dormitory for girls. I joined her there because she had enough stipends to pay for both of us. I also had a scholarship from the university that I gave to my mother.

In the dorm, I met a very nice friend, Chimi. Chimi studied PCB with me the same time, but she failed and was one year behind. Chimi was industrious, conscientious, and knowledgeable. She was very loving and caring. Sometimes when I was still in bed and we were having a bed check by the supervisor, Chimi would say, very excited, "Phùng Mai, wake up, go wash your face, let me make the bed for you fast. Hurry, they are coming!"

Out on a balcony looking down the street we used to study together while gossiping about our boyfriends and roommates. We often went shopping and Chimi had an eye for materials and fashion.

She would match a fabric with my complexion and judge, "You will look like a queen in that dress!" Often, I told Chimi I wanted to trade her more expensive brocade dress selections for less expensive dresses that were more practical for everyday wear. Chimi would happily said, "OK, do what you please, you are the queen!"

She was a dear friend, and I named my first baby after her.

### STARTING A FAMILY

My fiancé, Đệ, belonged to the Nguyễn Phước family when they were still the Viceroy, serving the Le dynasty, about three hundred years ago. I descended directly from Gia Long, the Viceroy who became the first Emperor of the Nguyễn Phước Dynasty. When De's parents came to my family to propose an engagement, my mother was afraid that this would not be permitted by the royal family regulation. She consulted with my uncle Ưng Úy whom I mentioned earlier. Ưng Úy was the minister of the Royal Family Affairs at that time. He said that if we go back up to the seventh generation of both sides and these two ancestors were not related, there would not be any objection. He checked the family trees on both sides and gave us permission to get married. We wanted to make sure that we were not consanguine for fear of genetic diseases in our offsprings. Some of our friends were very surprised that we could get married because both of us belonged to the Royal family!

We got married after graduating from the fourth year of pre-med, the most difficult year of them all. With her talents, Chimi matched my complexion with three yards of beautiful brocade to make my wedding dress.

We had our wedding ceremony at my brother Minh's house in Đà Lạt. My mother chose Đà Lạt to make it easier for my father to come from Sài Gòn. After the wedding, we travelled with my husband's parents to Qui Nhơn, then Huế, before returning to Sài Gòn.

We had our first child, Mimi, after we finished the fifth year of medical school. Dr. My was my obstetrician.

Thach was Mimi's babysitter. One day, when we came home from school, the land lady called me in and said, "I saw Thach carrying your baby in one arm and a butcher knife in the other, walking up and down the stairs! It was too dangerous!" I entered my house and saw Mimi in her crib and Thach sitting by, holding her bottle. I asked Thach how Mimi was. She said, "Mimi was very nice, eating good, happy, not crying." I asked her why she needed to carry the knife around.

She said, "To protect my baby from evil spirits." I was curious, "Who were the spirits?" She hesitated, "They are not real evil. They are my aunt and uncle. They were dead but they just came to visit me." I ventured, "Can I meet them?" She said, "Yes, they were behind the tree across the street. I will bring them in to talk with you." She went out, then returned, talking to the invisible people.

She asked them to sit at the table with me. I asked her to "interpret" my question, "What do they recommend?" She said, "They wanted me to return home for a while." I said, "Good, that's very wise and timely. Tell them that you will do what they desire. Now they can leave and be satisfied."

Thach saw her "spirits" through the door and when she returned said, "They have to go to a training class taught by Phùng Mai's fiancé, Đệ!" This was because when Đệ was my fiancé he always brought me inside, and watched me walking up the step to the dorm before he left. And when he came to pick me up, he would wait in the living room until I came to meet him. The other girls used to go out on the curb to wait for their boyfriends who would drop them at the other side of the street and leave. Chimi would say "Phùng Mai, hurry up, don't let Đệ wait. He might be mad at you!" I asked "Why hurry? If he cannot be patient with me for a few minutes, how can he be patient for the rest of his life?" Chimi exclaimed, "Phùng Mai, you are terrible!" I said, "No, I am not. Because I am sure that I wouldn't desert him for anybody else!"

I decided that Thach had an acute psychosis and told her "I will take you to see a doctor, a friend of mine. He dedicate some time with you to make you strong and healthy so that you can return to Huế with your family."

I took her to a well-known local psychiatrist who was an intern that taught us psychiatry about a year earlier. I introduced Thach and gave her history. He started treatments with a prescription for Mellaril.

Thach remained confused for a few days then recovered. When she was stable enough to take a train home, I gave her three months' salary that I kept for her. She was very happy and promised to return. Thach did return four months later. I asked her about the trip. She said after she bought the train ticket, she lost the rest of her money. "Maybe somebody stole it when I was asleep." I thought I was the crazy one to give all the money when she was not well. I should have given her only enough for the trip and kept the rest for her. I told her I was sorry, she said, "Never mind, Madam. I am happy, safe, and sound. Now I am back to thank you and serve you again."

I used her as a cook only thereafter, and I hired another babysitter for Mimi.

I made a very stupid decision when Mimi was about ten months old for which I have never forgiven myself. Mimi was very intelligent and outgoing. She was a happy and friendly child that would smile to everybody, even strangers. Đệ 's big sister, Linh, came to visit us. We went shopping and Mimi laughed and played with her aunt who was very excited. Mimi was especially happy when she saw other children running around. Linh bought her a beautiful stroller and her babysitter, Sau, took her out to play with the children in the neighborhood. Linh stayed with us for a few days, staying home with Mimi.

Every day, after we returned home in the evening, Linh would say, "Both of you go away all day, Mimi had nobody home to play with. Let me take her to Qui Nhơn with me. I stay home all day, and I can have my children play with her." I hesitated because Mimi had her babysitter, Sau, twenty-four hours a day. Linh insisted on letting her try for one month to take care of Mimi. She promised she would send her pictures weekly for me to see how happy Mimi would be. I thought my child would not miss me because she would have her babysitter, her aunt and uncle, and a whole house full of cousins in Qui Nhơn. I let her go with Linh and Sau was happy to follow. Mimi even smiled and waved good-bye to Đệ and me when the train left. I was more reassured that she would not miss me.

The first week passed by and there was no letter or photograph from Linh. I began to worry that Linh lied to me but my husband reassured that it took time to develop and send pictures. I waited for two more weeks and nothing happened. I told Đệ that we could not trust Linh with our baby because if she had to wait for the pictures, she could send letters instead. So, we took the train to Qui Nhơn. When we saw Mimi, she had lost weight. Linh said she did not cry but she would not eat. I asked, "Why you did not send pictures as you promised, or bring her back to me?" Linh said, "I was waiting for her to gain weight and to get used to her new environment." I knew that I had made a big mistake to let Linh care for my baby without my presence. We took Mimi home and she was again thriving, happy, and out-going. There was no sequela left from the forced separation.

I had my second daughter, Emmy, after I finished the sixth year of medicine. One week after Emmy's birth, I went to the printing shop every day to edit my doctoral thesis. After working for about three or four days, I could not stand straight because of pain in both hips. I thought I would never walk again. But with bed rest, vitamins, and calcium, I recovered in the same week. Again, I went to the printing office the following week to correct typographic errors because the printing clerk had difficulty with medical words. My thesis, written in French, was titled "The Normal Ocular Pressure of Vietnamese People." My husband at the same time was working in the military and did not need to complete a thesis.

In 1960 I presented my thesis and received my MD diploma, and moved to Huế when Emmy was one month old.

## CHAPTER XI.

### WORKING AT HUẾ GENERAL HOSPITAL

We lived at my maternal grandparents' home and opened an out-patient clinic in An Cựu, where I worked as a family doctor, mostly treating patients from the countryside. There I had three more children, Kiki, Miki, and Kiti. Our home was situated next to a military camp. My husband worked in another camp, about an hour's drive from home. He would come home at night on weekends. We had a cook, a nurse and three lived-in teenaged servants, all female, to care for our younger children.

**MY ADOPTED FOSTER CHILDREN AND WARDS**

One day, a woman from a distant village brought in a healthy ten-year-old-boy. She said she was encouraged by my sister's old wet nurse, Mụ Vú, to give me the boy for adoption. I asked "I have five children of my own. Why do I need to adopt one more?" The woman said, "Doctor, you have a big house and a large garden. You can raise many more children under your roof. Please, take my boy. He is a good boy. He can serve you. He can take care of your younger children." I said, "I already have three teenaged servants!" The woman pleaded, "Doctor, I will never forget your charitable heart to save my son because if I bring him back home, sooner or later, the Việt Cộng will get him!"

Surprised, I asked, "Why?" She explained through tears, "They are recruiting young boys and girls for carrying ammunition and supplies to the mountains! My son is too young for this. He will get sick and die if you don't save him!" I could not resist because she was telling the truth. I agreed to keep her son, Nhơn, after she wrote me an affidavit stating that if by bad luck, he got sick or died, it would be his destiny and she would not hold me responsible.

Nhơn's uncle soon brought to me an eleven-year-old girl named Khế and told me a similar story. Another woman from the nearby village brought in her twelve years old son Trung, after his father was just killed by the Việt Cộng. She too asked me to give her only son shelter.

I had a house full of children and "students" because I sent the foster children to a half day school, encouraging them to study hard. Khế would write a list of English or French vocabulary, stick it on the trunk of a jack fruit tree, and study while feeding Kiki after school.

During summer vacation, my husband's older brother, Đài, stayed with us for a few days. The students served him effectively. He asked me "How come so many wanted to give away their children to serve you so well? I wish I could have one to adopt. I would be very happy!" I remarked, "You have six children of your own. Why do you want more?" He said, "But our own children do not appreciate us for raising them. If we raise other people's children, they would appreciate and try to help and please us!"

I thought about it and that was true. I was very happy with all my foster children, but I knew Đài was a good man, so I arranged for him to adopt one. Out of the three, Trung, now fourteen years old, stood out. He was intelligent, cautious, and conscientious.

After I treated him for anemia from a hookworm infestation, I called him aside and said, "Trung, you are a good boy. You have helped me a lot; I am very proud of your behavior. Uncle Đài is the Dean of a junior high school. I want you to go live with him so that you can pursue your education and apply to the university. What do you think?"

Although he was a little sad, Trung replied, "If Madam wants me to go with Uncle Đài, I will obey." I reassured him, "Remember, I send you away to reward you, not because I don't want you by my side." He said, "I understand."

Đài was very happy to have Trung, who lived with him until he finished high school. Afterwards, Đài sent Trung to Sài Gòn to live with my other brother-in-law, Hịch, to finish his college in Agriculture.

The next summer, my sister Khánh Trợ, was transferred to Quảng Trị and she also needed help. I asked my students to see who wanted to follow Aunt Khánh Trợ. Khế volunteered. Khế lived with my sister and continued to graduate from high school and become a teacher before she married and moved out.

Later, a twenty-year-old cousin offered to serve me as a cook. She was an orphan, very intelligent, but never had an opportunity to go to school. I said, "I already have a cook, but I will send you to Khánh Trợ who will be very happy to have you and send you to school." She agreed to go live with my sister, and they became close friends.

Before I left Huế, another patient from Quảng Trị gave me her sixteen-year-old girl, Phien, to be trained as a nurse. Phien stayed with me for six months before I sent her back to Quảng Trị to live with my sister and continue her training. By the time my sister left Quảng Trị, Phien had become a full-fledged nurse.

## OUR PEACE DISRUPTED

One night, our peaceful living was shattered by the sounds of shooting, shelling, and grenade explosions. I feared they were attacking the military camp ten miles away, where my husband was serving as a captain. Đài was staying overnight and in response to the noise, threw himself and his only son to a corner while sheltering him with his own body. The next morning, we found out that our dog was killed in the kitchen from a stray bullet. In fact, the camp next door was attacked by the Việt Cộng. When my husband came home, we decided to move and live in Huế Hospital.

The hospital director gave us half of the first floor of a two-story building. My husband, Đệ, was displeased by this kind of treatment because both of us were serving Huế Hospital and deserved a larger place. He went to the Minister of Health and took the position of Hospital Director in a small province, B'Lao. He moved with our two older children, Mimi, and Emmy. I stayed with the rest, waiting to be transferred to B'Lao.

One summer night, the Việt Cộng attacked again with shelling and shooting. I again thought that they were aiming at the province chief's building next door, because they had no reason to attack a hospital. The next day, we found bullets and shrapnel! stuck into our walls and doors. One pig raised by our chauffeur who lived in the garage was killed. We decided to move to B'Lao quickly without waiting for a transfer.

# CHAPTER XII.

## MY EXPERIENCE IN B'LAO HOSPITAL

My husband had a scholarship to study public health in Amsterdam, Holland. The course lasted six months. I became the acting director of B'Lao's hospital. After he left for about two months, almost all the provinces in Việt Nam were attacked by the Việt Cộng. Only four or five provinces were not, and B'Lao was one of them. But we were fairly well prepared. The American MILPHAP team (Military Public Health Assistance Program) had made sandbags to pile up around their camp for protection. Mr. Smith from MILPHAP offered to help my family prepare for an attack. I asked them to do the same inside of our family room so that we would be protected by thick walls all around. Even then, we could be killed if a bomb fell from the roof, so I hired people to dig a trench underground close to the master bedroom. The top of the trench was reinforced by many additional layers of sandbags. Our family felt safer even though the attacks now felt like a certainty.

B'Lao province was made up of catholic villages and it was hard for the Việt Cộng to infiltrate, so they resorted to launching rockets. Tragically, one of these rockets landed close to the pagoda across the street from our home, killing four people from my friend's family: her husband and three children. During the attack, my friend knocked desperately for help, but we were inside the trench and couldn't hear her cries. We only found out about the devastating loss the next morning.

The "Tết Offensive" (Tết means the Chinese New Year) was catastrophic in Huế. The Việt Cộng infiltrated the population for some time and that day, many "regular" faces turned into communists. They arrested thousands of national officials, made them dig huge graves and buried them in mass.

Two friends of mine from Huế Hospital, Dr. Krainick and Dr. Ditcher, both originally from Germany, were killed. Mrs. Krainick chose to follow her husband when he was arrested and was also killed. I remember when Dr. Ditcher helped me prepare for my exam, the ECFMG in 1964. He had passed it himself and lent me his book to study. We received the news of his death two months later. The rest of my family moved to Sài Gòn from Huế, after the Tết Attack.

## TREATING MARASMUS LIKE MY MOTHER

After the New Year, an Irish doctor from Di Linh, a city about ninety minutes' drive from B'Lao, asked me to take one of his patients who was a twelve-year-old mountain boy. I went to Di Linh with Dr. Dolbee, Commander in Chief of the MILPHAP team, and Mr. Smith. The Irish doctor said, "This boy is cured of tuberculous meningitis. All blood tests and CSF (cerebral spinal fluid) values had returned to normal range. He was afebrile (no fever). But he would not eat and continued to lose weight. I didn't know what to do with him. He might die."

I examined the boy, he was another marasmus cachectic case with only skin and bones and two large hollow eyes, and a mouth full of teeth! He looked like a skinny bird with his arms and legs in flexion. His caseous bone stuck out like a tail. I had learned to treat marasmus when I was thirteen years old, watching my mother treated a cousin's infant, I told the Irish doctor "This is a challenge for me, and I will try. You can have him transferred to B'Lao Hospital." The patient's name was Katan.

I taught his family to give him warm baths in salt water. I talked with Bà Cúc, a woman laborer working in the maternity ward. Bà Cúc used to treat herself with placenta extract, using the placenta of healthy primipara with negative TB and VD tests. I told Bà Cúc to share her health food with the patient, Katan. I told Katan's mother to meet with Bà Cúc daily to get the "meat" for him. After she had the food prepared by Bà Cúc, she was instructed to season it with black pepper, onion, fish sauce and two teaspoons of beer. Who would place it in a bowl and steam it for about forty-five minutes. She would feed Katan with the tasteful juice of placenta extract, homemade.

I instructed his mother to feed him six times daily, every two to three hours with two to three teaspoonfuls of the juice. I watched him open his mouth and swallow his bouillon. He seemed to like it and would open his mouth for more. I was conservative and wanted to see his body react to it first. But he appeared to enjoy eating, not refusing to eat as described by his previous doctor who had saved his life. He would open his eyes, looking around, starting to recognize his mother's face and his surroundings. This was a twelve-year-old boy who had regressed into an infantile state after three months in semi-coma due to nervous TB. He could not sit up. He has forgotten how to talk and to smile. Thank God that he still remembered to swallow.

Progressively, I gave him more juice, brown rice soup, multi-vitamin. etc... I instructed his mother to add beer when the meat was almost done to retain the flavor. Katan began to make noise and smile. He had to say "coca, coca, coca" many times before he could have one teaspoon of food. Next, he had to say "eat meat, eat rice" to be fed. Gradually he learned to make sentences. He was able to sit up then to walk a few steps. The nurses and his mother would applaud him when he could do something new. After about three or four weeks, he was able to eat regular food with a huge appetite. But I still wanted him to continue with the placenta extract to speed up his recovery. I released him after two or three months and he gained about fifteen to sixteen pounds, able to walk, and to talk a little bit.

Two years later, when I visited the new hospital building built by the MILPHAP's grant, a nurse called out "Doctor, look at Katan, the boy we treated for marasmus! Now he looks like a young American, sixty-eight inches and one hundred sixty pounds!"

## TREATING THE BUBONIC PLAGUE

When my husband returned from Holland, he worked for the Red Cross. We made a fun trip to Đà Lạt where my brother Minh's family lived. We stopped at two or three places enroute to deliver free sewing machines and medicine to the villagers. He presided over some donation ceremonies given by the Red Cross.

After returning home, our youngest daughter, Kiti, had a fever. Kiti was about three years old at the time. I had Kiti sleep with us to monitor her sickness. The next morning, when I tried to carry her on my waist, her neck turned to one side. I asked her why she did not hold her head straight, and she said, "Mommy, it hurts." She showed me where it hurt, and I saw a tiny mark of an insect bit on her neck. I palpated for the lymph nodes, and they were swollen and painful. I told my husband that Kiti had the bubonic plaque and he examined Kiti and confirmed the diagnosis. He gave Kiti IV fluid plus chloromycetin IV drops and streptomycin IM. I observed Kiti for twenty-four hours. Her fever went down, and her nodes were less painful. After the first day, we stopped the IV and continued with IM and oral medicine. She recovered in less than one week.

I was surprised why spending a weekend in Đà Lạt could give Kiti the disease. Bubonic plague was endemic and sporadic in highland regions. I recalled that her babysitter did put Kiti down when we were watching the Red Cross donation in a small village between B'Lao and Di Linh. The tick carrying the plague must have jumped and bitten Kiti on the neck then.

After treating Kiti, I was more confident and experienced in treating other patients. People with bubonic plague refused to go to the hospital and asked me to treat them in my office. Some adult patients with one hundred- and four-degree temperatures who were carried on stretcher to my office in the morning were able to walk out of my office in the evening to return home. Some came back the next days on bicycles. I would treat them the same way as I had treated Kiti. They came back every day for about one week, until the danger was over.

In B'Lao, another family trusted me with their daughter, Truc, to help me in the office. Nhơn was nineteen, old enough to be trained to get vital signs and start an IV. He became an expert in starting an IV with a butterfly needle in children and with an intracath in adults. Truc also learned to provide routine hygiene and infectious control.

My husband and I were offered two positions as interns in a Lutheran hospital in Cleveland, Ohio. He was permitted to go for one year and I was not. Perhaps they were afraid that we might never return if we went abroad together. My husband decided to move the family to Qui Nhơn, close to his family, to help me supervise our children. I trusted Nhơn and Truc to bring most of our equipment by car, and we flew to Qui Nhơn. We waited for two weeks before Nhơn arrived. Truc explained that her father wanted to finish a wicker rocking chair to give me as a present and this had delayed their trip.

## CHAPTER XIII.

### MY PRIVATE PRACTICE IN QUI NHƠN

After my husband left to go abroad to Cleveland, Ohio in 1970, I became a single parent caring for five children alongside my practice in Qui Nhơn.

Emmy had just finished fifth grade while Kiki finished fourth grade in B'Lao. However, Emmy was too young to go to sixth grade and had to repeat the fifth grade. She argued, "I did good in fifth grade, why should I repeat it. I would rather stay home and wait until I am old enough to go to sixth grade!" Kiki said, "If Emmy is going to stay home, why should I go to school?" Their aunts and uncles had tried to reason with them, but they would not yield an inch. If they stayed home, they would fight each other, and it could be a disaster because both were very strong headed.

I had to find a solution and told Emmy, "Emmy, you are good, and everybody knows that you are a good student. Uncle Phong could not intervene here in Qui Nhơn to get you in sixth grade because of your age. But in Đà Lạt, your Uncle Minh and your cousin, Cam Van, had a good influence. I am sure that they could get you in. If you want, I will send you to Đà Lạt, a more modern resort town, and you will have lots of fun. I will stop by and visit you soon." Emmy agreed to go. With the same strategy, I talked Kiki into consenting to go to Sài Gòn to live with my brother Đích.

Mimi, Miki, and Kiti remained in Qui Nhơn. Mimi had to leave home before sunrise to go to school for physical education. I always sent somebody to walk to school with her in the morning for fear of her being kidnapped by strangers. She would come home around four or five in the evening with some friends.

One evening, Mimi did not show up on time. I ordered Nhơn to notify her aunts and uncles about her being late. They went out looking for her. When Uncle Phong arrived, he found Mimi finishing her needle work by herself in a classroom. Phong brought her home. It was the first time that I saw Phong being mad. He said, "Sister, you have to punish this girl. She cannot do that. She made the whole family worry!" I did not punish Mimi but only said, "Mimi, did you hear what Uncle Phong said? Do you know why he was so upset?" Mimi said, "I know. Everybody worried about me. I will not do it again. I am sorry, Mommy."

Another day, we could not find Miki. She was about five years old at the time and she had just played with some other children about half an hour ago. We looked around and across the street without seeing her. Miki was very popular. She was friendly with everybody, and people liked to carry her and play with her. Her Uncle Linh commented, "She acts like a man!" I asked "Why?" and he said, "Because Miki is not afraid of anyone!" A cousin went to a shoe store next door to look for her. She was playing with some teenaged girls upstairs!

I had to find a solution to this problem. Miki was too social, friendly, and free to be left alone with her older cousins. I asked Uncle Linh to send her and her sister, Kiti, to the Catholic boarding school twenty minutes away from home. They would go home on weekends so that I could supervise them when I did not have to work at the clinic.

## TREATING TETNAUS OUTSIDE THE HOSPITAL

I had a fairly good practice in Qui Nhơn with four to six maternity beds. I used some of the money to buy a house in Sài Gòn for my parents. My sister Khánh Trợ would go to Sài Gòn to help care for our elderly father.

For our family in Qui Nhơn, I bought a house for my parents-in-laws. At the time, my in-laws were living with my husband's sister, Linh. But according to the Vietnamese tradition, the parents should die in their son's home, not in a son-in-law's. I bought the house on Cường Để Street to make Đệ's parents happy, knowing that they could rest in peace in their son's home.

It was in this home on Cường Để Street that I treated an umbilical tetanus case for an outpatient. When the parents brought the one-week-old infant in, I told them my diagnosis and referred him to the hospital. But the parents said they knew the severity of the disease and that their infant only had a ten percent chance of survival. They begged me to treat the patient at home so that the whole family could take care of him. They said, "Doctor, we knew many cases like this who died in the hospital. If you treat him, there is some chance that he might survive. If you don't, we will take him home to let him die in peace with his family around."

The parents adamantly refused to take the baby to the hospital, and I could not let him die without being treated. I told them that I would keep him during the day and let him go home with his family at night. I talked with the New Zealand Medical Team who were assisting the hospital medical staff. They offered to supply the medication and equipment I needed to treat the case. The newborn infant was stiff as a board and would have a convulsion and pluck his lips at the slightest noise like a bump on his bed, or a honk of a car passing by. The IV medication was photosensitive and needed to be protected from light. I instructed the mother to sew a black cover to shield the bottle of IV drops. I stayed there all day caring for the infant in between seeing other patients. After sedation, the infant no longer had seizures and the antitetanic serum began to work. His neck was more supple and his body less stiff. He began to suck and swallow and no longer had a fever. I sent him home after about ten days and saw him for follow up every three to seven days. On his first follow- up, he developed oral candida albicans infection which was treated successfully. He recovered completely when he was two months old and was a healthy baby on his check-up.

The New Zealand Team, especially Dr. Neil was curious about the outcome. I told her about the success story, which was especially thanks to her help in arranging the medication and equipment. I organized a picnic for the team to celebrate the infant's recovery. At the picnic, Dr. Neil brought a memorable gift from her vacation in Hong Kong, a vacuum extractor as a souvenir from her travel.

By this time, Đệ had finished his internship and returned home because he did not receive an extension permitting him to stay another year. He later however checked with personnel and found out that he was permitted. So, he visited home for about a month then left again to start his first-year residency in Baltimore, Maryland. He returned from the United States at the end of 1972 and became the Medical Director of Qui Nhơn Hospital.

Truc left us in 1971 to return to B'Lao to take care of her sick mother. One of my dear clients who was a teacher introduced to me her special student, Oanh. Oanh was sixteen years old when she came to live with us. After three years, she married our foster child, Nhơn. Oanh had her first child in October 1974.

Our baby boy, Tivi, was born on June 1974. Before his birth, my mother had come to live with us as she was always there whenever my children were born.

# CHAPTER XIV.

## THE RETREAT TO THE SOUTH- VIA NHA TRANG, PHAN RANG, PHAN THIẾT, AND VŨNG TÀU

In February 1975, my husband took a course in Taiwan. Every day I received patients who came from the highland provinces. They reported that the Việt Cộng had invaded these provinces and the National troops had retreated. I was worried that Qui Nhơn would be taken and thought about moving south.

I visited with my niece, Cuc, who was the dean of a Qui Nhơn all-girls school. Cuc said, "I am moving to Sài Gòn today. If you don't leave now, you will get stuck." I stopped by Air Việt Nam to get tickets for Sài Gòn and they were all sold out for the next month. I met a friend, a doctor, who said, "If you don't escape, it's time for you to wash your feet, sit on the altar and eat bananas!" Oriental people used to offer fruits daily to the deceased. Laughing, I said, "No, I don't want bananas, I will find a way."

I stopped by my cousin, Bửu Khương, who was a colonel supervising army supply in Qui Nhơn. He said, "Phùng Mai, I think the Americans won't leave Việt Nam. They still have their bases in Da Nang and Cam Ranh. They won't desert us!" I listened to him talking in the background to his men, "Stick to colonel so and so, don't let him out of sight!" I thought to myself, "The situation seems more serious than he tried to reassure." I said, "Let me know when you retreat. I will come back again."

My last stop that day was to meet with Mr. Tuy, Chief of Public Works. Tuy's wife was my cousin. She was pregnant and was under my care. I told Tuy about my husband's leaving for Taiwan a week ago. He said if I wanted, he would send a truck and two chauffeurs to help me move which I accepted with gratitude. Tuy stated that his family would move to Nha Trang where his wife's brother-in-law had two commercial boats. We could use these boats to go to Sài Gòn. We scheduled a date to move together.

The next day, I came back to my cousin Colonel Bửu Khương's home. I saw all the preparation for moving. He said, "Phùng Mai, I believe we have to leave Qui Nhơn soon." I went to Tuy's home and told him about the military people deciding to retreat and we decided to move the next day.

## TO NHA TRANG

My mother (seventy-eight years old) had been living with us since Tivi was born at that time. Lily was Tivi's babysitter. Besides my mother and six children, I had Lily, Nhơn, Oanh and their baby, Robert moving with us. It was thanks to my mother, Nhơn, and Oanh, that we had a fairly comfortable exodus. Oanh was very intelligent and had an excellent memory.

On our way out of Qui Nhơn, Oanh said, "Madam, I think this time we will be defeated!" I asked, "How do you know?" She replied, pointing at a truck running by our side, "You see, national soldiers are wearing two layers of pants; civilian pants inside and military ones outside. This means when they see the enemy, they will throw away their guns and uniforms and become civilians. No combat!" I looked at the soldiers' legs and saw their civilian pants sticking out. I knew that Oanh was right!

When we were about to go through a narrow pass between two mountains, the traffic was packed, and we heard some shooting. Our driver stopped and walked forward to find out what had happened. He returned and announced, "Madam, they are fighting at the pass, our soldiers are disputing the right of way." I asked, "Did you get any instruction from your boss?" He said, "Before the departure, my boss has recommended: if they go, we go; if they stop, we stop; if they retreat, we will do the same!" I saw many cars and trucks making U-turn and driving back to Qui Nhơn. Others were still parking on the roadside. The driver asked "Madam, should we return?" I said, "No, we will wait. I think the soldiers will settle their dispute and the traffic will go through soon." After a few gunshot sounds, there was silence again. We waited for about half an hour and resumed our trip.

On our way to Nha Trang I picked up De's aunt's family of six people. We stopped at my cousin's home, Dr. Phan. Mrs. Phan led us to her unoccupied villa halfway from the seashore. There we rested and looked for a way to reach Sài Gòn. Every day, I went to Tuy's house, waiting for the boats to return. A few weeks passed by and there was no news about the boats.

The owner of the boats was my cousin's husband. He found out later that his boats were confiscated either by the government or by some military groups. I realized that in time of war, we did not "own" anything, even our lives!

## TO PHANG RANG

I decided to go to the next city, Phan Rang, by car. Tuy sent me a chauffeur who helped his family in Phan Rang.

While waiting, my elderly mother had diarrhea. Oanh gave her an IV and medication. Then it was Oanh's turn to have diarrhea and Nhơn gave her an IV. Oanh's baby, Robert, was about five months old; my baby, Tivi was eight months old. Everybody was in good health after a few days. Tuy was watching the Americans who lived next door. He said, "If the Americans are still here, playing basketball outside, we don't have to worry."

One day, I came to Tuy's house, and he announced "It's time for us to go now. Yesterday, the Americans were still there, but they left during the night!"

I went home and sent Oanh to go rent a vehicle for us to move as soon as possible. I told Oanh to use her good judgment to get a vehicle at any cost. Oanh returned and said a person had agreed to move us to Phan Rang and his car would be home that night. Oanh promised them a bonus if they showed up early. I suggested that either Oanh or Nhơn would wait at the owner's home until his car returned. They left and Nhơn came back stating that the car would be at our home around two o'clock in the morning.

I sent Tuy's chauffeur to drive our new car. I told my children to prepare for the departure and be ready at two o'clock. We had a safe trip to Phan Rang and my mother asked the chauffeur to stop at a temple in Phan Rang. She wanted us to stay there waiting for my husband to come. I told her we could not count on anybody in a time of war.

Many people stopped at the temple including a few military trucks. The monks in the temple stated that soon, they would move south by boats. Nhơn asked my permission to go to town to look for my husband's brother, Uncle Đài. Đài had lived in Phan Rang for the past eight years. He owned a Bata shoe store. I agreed for Nhơn to go to see if everybody else from Qui Nhơn had moved here.

Before, due to the disturbances our whole family did move to Nha Trang and Phan Rang for about two months in 1973 before returning to Qui Nhơn because "nothing has happened!" However, this time, felt different. My two children, Emmy, and Kiki, wanted to go with Nhơn and I agreed. This was a risky decision because they might get lost in the crowd. But naturally we would wait for them before we moved again. I told them to study the situation and come back soon.

That night, the monks' boat came and they were preparing to leave. Some of the refugees also left. My mother was scared and worried about the children who had not yet returned. Around midnight, we heard something which sounded like a helicopter. We thought that some officers were joining the military trucks. When the sound stopped, Kiki and Emmy ran in. They said that our relatives from Qui Nhơn came and stayed for one month and they just left this morning. Nhơn added, "Madam, if now we go with the soldiers, we would run the risk of getting robbed when we cross the forest. If we stay, we might get caught by the communists." I said, "No, we will go with the troops to town, and we will find a way, bus or boat, to go south. We will not cross the forest with them.

Then we left almost everything that we owned, including our new car, at the temple because we had no driver. We only took the minimum necessities and headed to town. Oanh succeeded in hiring a pushing cyclist for my mother and children to ride in the pick-up box, squatting on the floor. Nhơn and I rode on the side of a military truck. The traffic was heavy and there were many pedestrians. When we reached Đài's house, everyone was already had gone.

We went to the seashore to look for a boat to rent. We met my husband's sister, Linh, and her family who were returning from the seashore. They told us they were robbed by a group of soldiers. I decided to take the road to the next city, Phan Thiết.

## TO PHANG THIẾT

Nhơn went ahead to see if it was safe to proceed. He returned and gave me the gold that I had asked him to keep for me because I did not want to run the risk of being searched and robbed. Nhơn said, "Madam, I met a soldier who wanted to trade his shoes with mine because he did not want to look military. I told him that these shoes were given to me by my sister, and I go to ask her permission first."

Nhơn had the gold hidden in his shoes. I told him to give the gold to his wife, Oanh. Then he went to exchange his shoes with the soldier because this one was very nice and courteous.

We went back to Đài's house and his family also came back there, because they could not find a boat. I gathered all my husband's brothers and sisters' families to go with me. Counting our family, we had about forty-five to fifty people together. We all walked south with a crowd of other people from Phan Rang. My nephew-in-law asked me to cover my face with a scarf so that nobody could recognize me. After about a half hour walk, my children started to leave behind the bicycles because nobody wanted to ride it slowly with the crowd.

Nhơn carried a large suitcase containing important documents, diplomas, and some valuables. He told my children, "You may throw away your clothes if you don't want to carry them. Mommy will buy new ones for you when we reach another town. But I need to carry mommy's stuff." I felt bad for Nhơn that he had to carry my heavy belongings. I told him, "Let us keep only the valuables. You may throw the rest away if it is too heavy."

Nhơn said, "No, Madam. Everything in the suitcase is important. You may need your papers to practice. I am OK, don't worry." He was right. All my life, I did not pay attention to documents. I always thought I could get a duplicate at the university if I lost my certificates. I even did not bother to get my diploma after I graduated from PCB college. If Nhơn had not packed all the important documents he found in my husband's drawers before we left Qui Nhơn, I would have lost all our diplomas, including our ECFMG certificates and our internship contracts to work in the U.S.! And Nhơn did protect the documents that he had saved for us.

We also carried about one gallon of drinking water, mostly for the babies, Tivi and Robert. Nhơn suggested, "Madam, you don't have to worry about Tivi; Oanh can breast feed both of them if we get stuck in a forest!" I said, "No, we will find a bus to ride south."

There were no buses going our way. People set a fire at a gas station back in Phan Rang, possible for a personal revenge. A man from the crowd recognized me and told his wife "Honey, look! The doctor also had to walk, and you complained continuously about having to hike!" His wife was one of my patients.

Since there were no buses, cars, or trucks going south, I told Nhơn to start stopping the buses coming from the south. I told him to stand in the middle of the road to flag them down, and to tell the bus drivers that everybody was going south. I told Nhơn to tell them that they should turn around and go back south and we would pay for the whole trip. I also reminded Nhơn to tell them that people had burned some gas stations in the city, and they would not be able to get gas to go north.

My sister-in-law, Đài's wife, stated that she and her children were tired of walking and they wanted to stay where they were instead of proceeding. I told her "No, you and the children just try to walk a few more miles. I am sure that Nhơn can find us an empty bus." A moment later, Nhơn had succeeded in convincing a driver to turn around going north for us.

When the bus stopped, we all boarded and found our seats. When I got on the bus, my children had to make a seat for me. Linh asked me to pay for the trip, promising that they would reimburse me later, which they never did. The bus stopped halfway to rest. Tivi was thirsty and started to cry. Nhơn had to get water for him from a spring. Some relatives still had bottled water with them, but they did not offer us any, saving it for themselves. I noticed this when some of them drank bottled water after the bus started again.

As the bus drove its way to town, we saw passing by the window, a woman wounded from an altercation. We stopped at the next northern town, Phan Thiết, and took refuge in a temple. After our stop, Nhơn and Oanh cooked dinner for our family and we ate before dark. When the night came, we heard tirade of machine guns and hand grenade explosion. We thought that the communists were invading the town. It turned out that it was our soldiers who shot at the iron gates of different stores to loot merchandise that the store owners had left behind.

## TO VŨNG TÀU

During the shooting, Nhơn asked my permission to go look for a boat. I said, "Don't go yet. They are still shooting; you might get shot!" He said, "Madam, I believed you are blessed by Buddha and always have good luck. I cannot get shot because if I get wounded while I am serving you, it would turn out that you were not blessed and lucky! I believe I will be safe because of your virtues, generosity, and charitable heart!"

Nhơn had bet his life on my good luck and insisted on going. I told him to avoid the crowd and go to the fishing village to get a boat to go to Vũng Tàu, a southern resort near Sài Gòn. My mother was touched by Nhơn's sacrifice and fidelity and prayed for him to be safe and successful. I also prayed that he would be back soon.

Nhơn returned after an hour and said that a family agreed to let us rent their boat. I asked Ky, my husband's brother-in-law, and Phong, my husband's brother, to go with Nhơn and negotiate the price. The price was set at half a million or forty ounces of gold. Dai's wife gave me her golden ring as her contribution to the cost. Later, since no one else reimbursed me for the cost of the trip, I returned the ring to Đài's wife.

When the shooting ceased, we started to go to the village by the seashore. I entered a lady's home. She invited my whole family in and cooked for us a big meal. She said, "I sympathize with all of you. You must eat and not be hungry. Nobody knows what may happen out there in the sea. You might be buried in the fish's stomach!" It was raining hard, and the wind was blowing. I asked, "Is the sea very bad tonight?" She said, "Not quite, but sometimes the wind turns to be high."

I went to the boat owner and told him I wanted to be safe. If he thought that tonight was not safe for the trip, we would wait until the sea was calm! The owner said, "My ship costs four million. Do you think I would risk my life and my ship for half a million to go out in a bad sea?" I was reassured by his reasoning and experience.

We set a schedule to leave after midnight that night, hoping that other refugees would still be asleep and would not hitchhike our boat. I was worried that too many people would sink the boat! I told the owner, "I want this trip totally for my family. I will pay the whole price for it. Do not take any other people." And he agreed.

After midnight, we started boarding the boat in small groups for fear of being noticed by the other refugees. The boat had a smaller second floor which belonged to the crew. Everybody else sat on the main floor. After about fifteen minutes of navigating, I lay down to rest. A strange male voice came from the first floor, "Are you afraid, sister?" I looked up and was very scared. I felt cold in my spine and goose bumps on my skin. I saw a man with a mustache in his late thirties. I was thinking about pirates but the way he addressed me was nice and courteous for a pirate. I was reassured and responded in a matter of fact yet honest tone, "Yes, I am. Since when did you board? I did not see you?"

I did not know him, but I sounded very friendly like I knew him. He said, "Before midnight. I waited here for two hours before your family came!" I asked, "Then, you are going to Vũng Tàu with us?" and he said yes and wished me good luck. I thanked Buddha for not meeting a wicked man. I guessed he also paid for his trip before we rented the boat, or else he was a relative of the crew, although he talked with Huế dialect. But I did not ask.

People started getting seasick and vomiting. Every time somebody made a sound of vomiting, eight-month-old Tivi laughed happily, thinking they were playing with him. At first people vomited overboard but later they just did it on the floor. My mother, lying down, was soiled by the vomitus. Her skin got irritated and red. We could not do anything about it until we reached our destination. People continued to vomit as Tivi laughed. Oanh, Lily, and I were amused and laughed with him. We were thankful that Tivi did not get seasick. Lily held him, face up, in her arms. When we had a rough wave, salt water splashed on the floor and flew into his face but he did not cry. I told Lily to hold him sitting up. I was pleased that nobody cried or complained.

We reached Vũng Tàu the next day and settled temporarily on the beach with other people. Nhơn got fresh water for my mother to wash herself and bought food for us. We were excited to see Vũng Tàu (meaning the gathering of boats).

My sister-in-law, Linh, began to cry and moan, "Other people were able to bring their children and servants, and I could not even bring my two sons, Lu and Ki." I asked her where they were. She replied, "They rode a motorcycle ahead of us and disappeared in the crowd!" I told her, "Stop crying. They are young and resourceful. I bet that they would be in Sài Gòn before us! If you could not find them, I would give you ten ounces of gold or you could have this trip free of charge!"

Then De's other sister, Thuyên, had a verbal altercation with Đài's second wife, Sương. Sương complained that she had to care for her three children without their father, Đài. Thuyên had a nomadic husband who had never been home, and two teenaged daughters who she had been caring for by herself for years. Thuyên felt that she had the right to complain, but not Sương. Thuyên challenged, "Why don't you grab Đài's shirt and follow him, with your children." When I came close to them, they stopped arguing.

A teenaged niece asked me, "Auntie Đệ, why did you never have a problem like everybody else?" I smiled, "I also have problems, but I solve them in a peaceful way." Indeed, all my family had a good time during the escape because they had trust in me and my helpers, Nhơn and Oanh. All my children knew not to cause problems, and stopped arguing or teasing each other, during the emergency. I felt blessed that the situation felt under control at all times except when I saw that unexpected passenger on the boat!

# CHAPTER XV.

## THE REUNION IN VŨNG TÀU

After we ate and relaxed, Nhơn called a taxi to take us to a temple on my mother's suggestion. Accompanied by my sister, Phùng Khánh, a Buddhist nun, my mother had visited many of the temples in Vũng Tàu. She did not know the name of this specific temple, but she instructed the taxi driver to drive us to a "well known, beautiful temple up on the mountain, looking down at the sea." The driver had an idea of the place my mother had in mind, but for me any temple would be fine as I knew we would be welcomed thanks to my sister's great connections.

The driver asked, "We have two temples like that. Which one do you want to go to? The one on the front beach or on the rear beach?" I asked, "Which one is less busy and more peaceful?" He replied the one near the rear beach and I told him to go there.

Later, Nhơn told me that he met Tuy's chauffeur at the market. The chauffeur told him that Tuy had been robbed of all his gold and money. I felt sorry for my benefactor who had helped us move.

We had a good time staying at the temple. I planned to stay there for a few months because it would be convenient to leave from there if we wanted to travel abroad. I was sure that Nhơn and Oanh could find out a way to go from Vũng Tàu. We were waiting for my husband who should have been back in Sài Gòn by now.

After his return from Taiwan, Đệ sent a telegram to my nephew, Dr. Vinh Luc, who worked in Nha Trang Hospital. Vinh Luc gave me the telegram. Luc was Dr. Phan's son-in-law, whose house we had stayed in Nha Trang when we came there. I did not know how to get in touch with my husband in Sài Gòn. I decided to take my family to Sài Gòn to meet him there.

Đệ learned about people from Qui Nhơn and Nha Trang having left town to move south. He asked our relatives in Sài Gòn if they had heard anything about us, but nobody knew where we were. He learned that many people came to Vũng Tàu as refugees. So he came to the Minister of Health and volunteered to go to Vũng Tàu to help the refugees.

Đệ looked up all the refugee camps in Vũng Tàu and could not find us. He never realized that we were relaxing in a temple looking down at the beach. Very disappointed from his fruitless search he started to leave Vũng Tàu for Sài Gòn. But, when he was riding in a jeep on his way back, suddenly his brother Phong saw him and yelled out his name. He was so relieved to see his brother and asked Phong about us and Phong told him where we were.

While I was fixing dinner, my children ran up from the beach yelling, "Mommy, Mommy, Dad is here!" Then I saw Đệ following them with a big smile.

I asked if he knew about the coming war before he left for Taiwan. He said, "I suspected it, but I thought if I left, you could get out of town easily. If I had stayed, I would be stuck to the hospital until the last minute and all our family would have a hard time to get out!" Although he never admitted, he did believe that I was always resourceful and lucky. In a way I was glad that we ran from the war without him because he would be very tense, nervous, and we would risk making the wrong decision if he was there.

Our family went to Sài Gòn the next day, but my mother wanted to rest at the beautiful temple a bit longer. She said she would go to Sài Gòn when it was more peaceful.

When we arrived in Sài Gòn at my brother-in-law Hịch's house, we received the bad news that just the night before, my father had just passed away.

Đệ went back to Vũng Tàu to bring my mother to Sài Gòn.

# CHAPTER XVI.

## GOING TO SÀI GÒN AND FINDING A WAY TO LEAVE VIỆT NAM

We stayed at my father's house with my sister, Khánh Trợ, and her four sons. They had been taking care of my father since his stroke two years earlier. I came on time to look at his peaceful face before they closed the coffin.

Đệ and my mother came the next day. My father had a nice funeral even in war time, thanks to my two sisters Phùng Khánh and Phùng Thăng (known as Trí Hai and Huế Minh by the Buddhist nuns). All our family went on a vegetarian diet for forty-nine days to pray for the deceased's soul to be free and happy. I also prayed for us to get a way out of Việt Nam.

Our son, Tivi, happened to have diarrhea for many days. I guessed he was infected when he had to drink the water from the mountain spring. Đệ had to change the medication two or three times before Tivi recovered from his sickness.

One day, Oanh and I were working on the green vegetables on the floor. Tivi sat nearby and put something in his mouth. I asked him to open his mouth and there was a green worm lying on his tongue. I was so surprised that he saw the worm because we did not see it. I took it out of his mouth and called my mother who was sitting on a couch nearby. "Mama, Tivi saw a worm, picked it, and put it in his mouth!" My mother laughed, "Let me see the worm!" When I looked down to show her the worm, it was not there. It was back in Tivi's mouth and this time he stuck out his tongue to show us that he had the worm, smiling!

His brother, Kiki, came and attempted to "punish" him. Kiki made Tivi stand against the wall, facing out, since he could not yet stand up by himself. Tivi was very afraid to fall and he urinated on the floor. Everybody laughed. Tivi's sisters tried to repeat the test and Tivi urinated again. I told my children "You cannot test him anymore. He is scared and loses control of his bladder. It is cruel to repeat the test." They said, "but he did not cry and did not fall! He is not afraid; he just urinates to get out of trouble!" I was not sure about my theory because Tivi himself did not look very distressed.

A few weeks later, a fire broke out in our neighborhood. We placed the children and valuables in a jeep and went across the street. We rested at a friend's house. There I saw American and Korean men going in and out talking to their families. I thought about paying a family to accept us as parents or siblings so that we could get out of Việt Nam.

The fire was put out before it reached two houses from ours, and we returned home. I saw in the newspaper the photograph of the U.S. ambassador in Cambodia who was rolling the American flag to go home. I thought to myself, "Sài Gòn will be taken over by the communists soon."

## PLANNING OUR LEAVE

My husband was busy looking for a house for us to move out of. He already took a job at Hùng Vương Hospital near Chợ Lớn. He took me out to look at two houses for sale. We agreed to buy a house close by his work and he insisted on paying the down payment. I talked with the owner who told me that they would be moving to a province in the south. But I saw that the family was in the process of sewing individual carry-ons. I know that they were lying because if they were moving to the province, they did not have to do all this preparation!

I told my husband what I had thought and advised him not to pay the down payment yet. He did not believe me and insisted on paying because he was afraid that they would sell the house to somebody else! A few weeks later, while we were standing in line to board the plane to go to America, we saw this family a few steps behind us!

My sister Khánh Trợ received a telegram signed by Kissinger, regarding a mass evacuation. Her ex-husband PD Tai had already sent papers sponsoring his mother, his brother La, and each of his children. Tai advised his family to prepare to go when they received the Kissinger's telegram. I told my sister "There is no way that La would go without his wife and children! Each sponsoring paper would serve to sponsor a whole family!"

My nephew, Tú Anh, began to type our names under his sponsoring paper. He asked me to let his friend, Thanh, to be on our list. I said, "Why not? If we can go, he will go with us." Tú Anh photocopied many lists for us to use in case of loss.

Tú Anh had an American friend who was a journalist. He brought this friend home and we talked. I asked him what do the American mean about "mass evacuation" and "humanitarian aid?" He said, "I guess that about six hundred thousand Vietnamese could go to the U.S. as refugees and that the funding for the military operation now becomes the charitable aid for the refugees." I was very hopeful that we could go.

I told my husband and he said, as always, "You don't know anything about politics! This is not the case!" I asked, "Then, what do you think is right? And what do you know?" He remained silent and sullen, and I left him alone. I decided to do things on my own without discussing with him.

Luckily, Đệ went to work every day and I had plenty of time for planning. I decided to go with the journalist to the U.S. Embassy in Việt Nam. He came at night, and I waited until midnight when my husband was sleeping and rode with him on the back of his motorcycle. He rode very fast. Each time he stopped at a streetlight, he managed to pass the intersection before the traffic. I was scared but did not say anything.

When we reached the Embassy, thousands of people were standing in many lines, waiting for the gate to open. Some even attempted to climb the wall in front of the building. I thought I could not get close to any Embassy personnel through this chaos. I saw some people waiting at the bus stop to go to the airport and proceeded to wait with them. I asked the journalist to leave me there and I would go home later.

When the bus came everybody got on. I had no paper to ride the bus and hesitated, afraid that the driver would tell me that I was not allowed. The driver looked out and said, "What are you waiting for? Come on, board the bus quickly. I must drive one hundred people to the airport each hour!" I said I was sorry to make him wait and got on the bus.

I guessed that the driver had received the order to drive to the airport anybody who waited at the bus stop across the street from the Embassy. Other people who were waiting at the gate around the Embassy building probably did not know about this!

The bus went directly inside the Tân Sơn Nhất Airport without being stopped at the gate for questioning or searching. Once inside the airport, I walked around, observing, to find a way for my family to go to America.

I walked with the people who stopped by the gym, the bowling alley, etc... up to the swimming pool to have their papers checked. I had my papers with me, but I would wait for my family. After learning the protocol of moving from the airport gate to the swimming pool where people were waiting to go to the planes, I took a taxi home.

My family was still asleep except for my mother who knew that I was out. I told her about my adventure and said that I would go to the airport a few more times to get my papers signed to go to the U.S. She said that after we were settled in America, she would join us. In contrast to my husband, my mother was very optimistic and had always trusted me.

## THE PAPERS

The next day, my sister and her family were ready to go to the airport to leave for America. I accompanied them to study the situation again. This time, their bus was stopped at the gate by the police.

Two officers entered the bus asking the adult males to show their papers. My youngest nephew, Thiên Tứ, had no papers because he was a soldier who was reported killed in the battle. When he returned to town, he decided not to rejoin his unit, allowing the army to believe that he was dead!

On the bus, Tú Anh argued with the officers. They arrested him and all the family descended the bus with Tú Anh. Only my sister's "adopted daughter," Soa, whom she trusted with her gold and papers in a bag, remained on the bus and left for America with my sister's papers.

During the verbal altercation with the police officers, Thiên Tứ managed to walk away without notice. I found out that Tú Anh arranged the "smokescreen" for Thiên Tứ to escape! The police let my sister go to the station with her three sons. I was left behind to decide a way to get them out.

I walked up and down the street and noticed a motorcyclist who was riding in and out of the police station gate. I stopped him and asked for a ride to the gate. It turned out that he was a policeman himself who was moonlighting by transporting passengers. I asked him how I could get my nephews out. He said, "Sister, don't worry. Any SOB colonel could do the job, no big deal!" I learned that people despised our high-ranking officers by calling their names while knowing that they still had some powers! I also learned that I could hire a policeman to bring my husband in the airport.

I went home and repeated the funny statement of the policeman/motorcyclist. Thiên Tứ was already home. He said, "Uncle La is the damned Colonel!" He went with my sister Phùng Khánh to look for Uncle La to release his brothers who were in detention.

I took Emmy and Kiki to the airport when my sister's family went the next time. There were no obstacles, and I accompanied my sister's family to the gym waiting for their turn to go. Tú Anh introduced me to an American Admiral. He knew the officer's rank because he had studied in America in 1960 for one year when he was about sixteen years old. The Admiral asked to see my papers and he signed them. We went to the swimming pool to see people boarding the airplane. An American Colonel saw me and my two children. He told us to board the plane. I said, "Thank you, but I have to go get my husband and my other children first."

I took Emmy and Kiki directly to Hùng Vương Hospital to meet my husband. Upon seeing Đệ, Emmy yelled out, "Daddy, we got the paper signed!" A nurse asked Đệ, "Doctor, are you going to America?" He said, "No, we are going to the province." Just like the homeowner who lied to us.

# LEAVING

We went home and prepared to go. Đệ told the children to bring only two changes of clothing each in small bags. He said if we brought large suitcases, the police might stop us and cause problems. We also brought another nephew, Bae, to the airport.

At the gate, the police stopped our taxi and asked the men to step down. They said that all males in the age of military draft could not enter the airport without a permit. Before Đệ and Bae had to return home, I told them to wait at the same corner around four and I would find a way to let them in.

In the airport, I saw the same taxi driver bringing people in. I approached the driver to get some information. He said that he had a contract with the police to help transport people who were allowed to leave by the Americans. I made a deal with the taxi driver to meet me at four so that I could bring my husband and nephew with us this time. I promised to pay him double after he did the job.

Around three o'clock, we saw Đệ walk up with Hịch and Kim Thu, his youngest brother and sister-in-law. Thu said she stopped by our house earlier and only saw my mother sitting on the couch. She looked in and left, disappointed because we were gone. Oanh happened to walk out of the kitchen and saw Thu. She called out "Auntie, my master is still here! He is doing something behind the altar!" Oanh could not go with us because she had to wait for her husband, Nhơn.

Nhơn had insisted on returning to Phan Rang to bring in all our belongings and the car that we had left there. When we had the opportunity to go to the U.S., Oanh told me, "Madam, bring Lily with you so that she could help you. My son, Robert, and I cannot go because we have to wait for Nhơn." It was thanks to Oanh who was very smart and loyal that my husband could go with Kim and Hịch to the airport that day.

Hich bought tickets to go to a province to get to the airport. Somehow his car happened to be behind two American jeeps. The gate keeper thought his car belonged to the group and let them enter the airport without checking.

My sister's family had already left. She gave me a letter to give to the American consulate. She had a habit of writing letters to thank the officials in charge when they had helped her with something. She would not care if the official knew her or not. All she would do was to introduce herself and her family, brief him about how he did help her, etc... I had her letter, thinking it would be nice to show somebody your gratitude, and decided to give it to the consul if I met him.

Tú Anh, her oldest son, was worried that my family did not get to go yet. He said, "In case you could not go by air, you just stay in the airport and American helicopters would lift you to take you to the American seventh fleet on the Pacific Ocean." He was so sure that it reassured me a lot.

When my husband walked in with his brother, Hich, and his wife, Kim Thu, Kim was very excited to tell me about her adventure. She talked about how they went to look for a way out and how, thanks to Oanh, that she could meet my husband and come with him. I told Kim and Hich about what Tú Anh told me that they just needed to bring their family into the airport and the American would help them out of Việt Nam. I gave Kim a copy of our papers of sponsorship sent by Tú Anh's father. I explained that Tú Anh was sponsored but he had to bring his family with him and we were Tú Anh's aunt, uncle and cousins as explained in the list. I suggested that Kim would add a list of names of her family under Tú Anh's name when asked for a signature. Kim was very hopeful that her family could go with us.

That evening, we stood in line to present our papers to proceed toward the swimming pool, which was the last stop. I was disappointed because the people before us presented many papers such as marriage and birth certificates of all the family members. We did not have those papers with us. Besides, after checking the papers, the sergeant sitting at the table just signed his name and stamped under the list! Our list was signed by a Colonel without a stamp! I was afraid that the sergeant would not approve our papers, and it was true. When we presented our papers, he told us that they were incomplete, and he wanted to see the birth certificates of the children which we did not have.

We had to step aside so that he could proceed to check the person next in line. While waiting to figure out a way to get our papers stamped, I heard someone yell out, "You are killing me. You letting my family get killed!" It was the accusation of a desperate man who was just got rejected by another sergeant, at a table nearby. After this emotional outburst, his family were allowed pass! I said to myself "Oh no! I hope that we could get our papers approved without protest!"

## THE VICE CONSUL

Đệ and I went to another building and asked to talk to the American consul. We were told to go upstairs. We met two American men, one of them beckoned us to follow him. Out of anxiety and excitement, we followed the wrong man. He was tired and grumpy and asked us, "Why do you follow me? the other guy was the one that wanted you!" We were relieved and apologized in a hurry, "We are sorry!" while the other man turned back and showed us his office, "This way!"

After sitting down behind his desk, he asked "How can I help you?" Đệ showed him our papers "We need your approval because the official downstairs would not validate the Colonel's signature. Please help us. We are both doctors and had contracts to work as interns at the Lutheran Hospital in Cleveland, Ohio. We can sponsor ourselves. We will not be a burden for the Americans."

The Vice Consul (I found out later that what he was) took our paper, signed it, and put his stamp on it. I said, "Sir, my sister sent you this letter." He read the letter and asked "Where is your mother and your younger sisters? Are they coming, too?" I said, "They decided to go at a later time!"

We thanked him for his favor, "You have saved our family. I will never forget."

He said, "When you go to the United States, try to help the poor Americans."

And I promised him that we would.

We did not remember the name of our benefactor, but we hoped some day we could find out and renew the contact. However, we kept our promise to help the poor by working mostly with the state hospitals and seeing mostly Medicaid and Medicare and SAMI (State Assistance for Medically Indigent) patients in our private practice. I even told some of my patients about our promise to the American Vice Consul in April of 1975.

We joined our family and again stood in line to proceed. My husband glanced at the stamp on the other people's paper and said, "How come their stamps are so big, but ours is small! I am afraid..." I interjected" Stop worrying! We have gotten the Vice Consul's signature. Our paper must be valid!" And it was. After seeing our papers, the sergeant let us pass.

Tú Anh's friend, Thanh, joined us and we rode in a pick-up truck to reach our last stop before boarding the airplane. We passed some Vietnamese soldiers and police officers. Thanh bent his head and hid it behind his crossed arms. Đệ was surprised that Thanh was so cautious. He thought that once we were transported by the Americans, we were safe.

That was not the case. The Vietnamese police and officers still had the right to stop the vehicle and check the men's papers!

We only felt safe after the airplane took off.

# CHAPTER XVII.

## ON THE WAY OUT OF VIỆT NAM AND LIVING AS REFUGEES

We first stopped at an airport in the Philippines and received food and drink from a charity before flying to Guam. We stayed with a dozen other families in a large house that looked like a warehouse. There were no partitions, only two scattered rows of columns with a makeshift aisle in the middle to walk through. Each family in proportion to their size, occupied a space along a wall. Our family of ten, including Thanh, huddled together in a space equal to three king sized beds.

After we were settled overnight, the next morning Kim Thu walked in. Laughing, she said, "I knew that I could find you here somewhere!" We were so glad and excited that they could get out of Việt Nam and join us so soon!

Hịch and Kim Thu had three small children: Tybel, Telby, and Belty. They were four, three, and two years old, respectively. We made a place for them on the right side of our lot. Kim told us the story about how she could get to the airport with the paper we gave them. Kim reported how sorry she was to have left Hịch's mother behind. But they were happy that they had time to give their belongings to their family.

I asked about the car LaDalat which we sold to them after we bought our new car. Kim said it was left at the airport. I commented "What a waste! Why did not you give it to your brother?" Kim said, "There was nobody around. No one could escort us to the airport." But they said they were still happy for anybody who could use their car. Kim said, "The LaDalat had served us plenty! Thanks to it that we could drive brother Đệ and our family to the airport." She had no regrets even though they only owned it for less than four months.

It was very noisy and chaotic in the compound. People would announce on the microphone their arrivals and their search for old friends and relatives "Mrs. or the Colonel so and so wants to know her friend so and so's whereabouts! Please contact building number...etc." Đệ was irritated by the way they addressed each other. He commented, "They already forgot that now they are refugees, no longer colonels or generals..." I disagreed; the titles were their identification. If they didn't call by the titles, how could they recognize their friends or relatives by names, because many people had the same name! Still, I saw it as a way of holding on to your old life, and in a way my husband was right. Now, as refugees, everything was going to change.

Tybel, Hịch oldest son was very special. He was used to the easy life and could not cope with the emergency move and chaos. He was grumpy, demanding, and whining. Suddenly, I heard a slap and a yell, "Stop whining, be quiet!" And Tybel immediately stopped crying. Everybody froze to a standstill. It was Đệ who disciplined Tybel. I looked at Hịch and Kim, and we understood each other. After this incident, all the children were very quiet and happy. They knew that they could not use the chaos as an opportunity to be out of line.

There was an epidemic of pink eyes in the compound and I caught it. Đệ bought for me grapes and other fresh fruits. He and the children did not eat the fruits because he said, "Save them for mommy who is sick!" I do not remember if I had shared the fruits with my family or not, but I felt very entitled to this special treatment.

We had public television on the camp. In April, the thirtieth, one week after we left Việt Nam, we learned the news that the Vietnamese Communists had taken over our country.

We lost our country while we were in Guam.

## REFUGEE CAMPS IN THE UNITED STATES

Belty was sick and had a fever before we left Guam for the United States. We stopped in Hawaii for a few hours then flew to San Francisco. Belty had measles and was hospitalized in Hawaii. We continued our flight to San Francisco without Hịch's family. We stayed overnight in San Francisco before we were sent to different camps in California and Arkansas. While stopping in San Francisco, we were led to a camp with a row of houses built side by side. I went ahead of my family, noticed a clear and empty one and asked the guide if my family could stay there. He had no objection and we settled in. Other people in the same group went past our house with their guides.

The following morning, the other group was sent to Camp Pendleton in California and our family was sent to Fort Schaffe, Arkansas. Due to this choice of housing, a few days later Hịch's family could join us in Fort Schaffe after Belty recovered from measles. Hịch was happy that we could stay in the same camp.

At Fort Schaffe, we lived upstairs in a two-story building. Our family had one large room with many bunk beds. We placed the beds together in groups against the walls to prevent the children from falling. We ate in a mess hall after standing in line to get our food. This reminded me of poor people in Việt Nam standing in line to receive charity from the nuns in the pagoda.

Our children suggested, "Mommy and Daddy, you don't have to stand in line. We will do it for you. You just stay home, and we will bring the food home for you." A friend of ours, Dr. Bui. visited us in our dorm and saw us eating a nice meal with rice, chicken, and vegetables. Mrs. Bui asked "How come you could get so much meat on your plate? They only gave us a few!" I then realized that our children had saved their food for us. I understood deeply the profound meaning of this saying, "you only know your loyal officer when there is trouble and your piteous child when you are poor."

One day, Thanh announced that the Salvation Army was distributing clothing for people who needed it. Thanh went with my children to get some. He brought back for me a dress and asked me to try it on. He laughed happily when he saw that it fit me and I looked very nice wearing it. This reminded me of Nhơn and Oanh who were very excited when Oanh brought back clothing for me to try on from the store.

Then it was Tivi's turn to get sick. He had a fever for many days and coughed up pink phlegm. Lily and I woke up early when it was still dark to take him to the hospital. The fever and the cough did not abate until the measles broke out. Apparently, a little girl who lived in the next room also had the measles. After the measles, Tivi had diarrhea for many days and we again went to the hospital early to get special formula for him.

A few weeks later, we were visited by Dr. Niem who let Đệ know that some American people were recruiting doctors for their community. I got the news that Mr. and Mrs. Stanley in California wanted to sponsor our family. Mr. Johnson from Wilmot, Arkansas, wanted to recruit Đệ to work in their outpatient clinic. Dr. Bui already accepted a position and left For Schaffe for Wilmot, Arkansas. We were trying to decide between going to go to California or Arkansas. I wanted to go to California and contacted Mrs. Stanley. Đệ talked with Dr. Bui regarding the conditions in Wilmot. He told me that Bui said it was very nice, just like a fairy tale! When I went to the community room to talk to Mrs. Stanley on the phone, Mr. Johnson was listening and interrupted, "We are hiring her husband for 35-40 thousand dollars a year, you should take this into consideration!" Mrs. Stanley told me to choose where I wanted to go. I discussed it with Đệ and we decided to go to Wilmot, Arkansas.

# CHAPTER XVIII.

## SETTLING IN THE UNITED STATES, WILMOT, ARKANSAS

After two months of living in the refugee camp at Fort Schaffe, Mr. Johnson picked up my husband and our three older children and drove them to our new house in Wilmot. I flew with the smaller children in a small airplane owned by a rich man in the community. Đệ recalled that they drove a long way and they stopped at a steak house for lunch.

On the way, they passed through some small county roads bordered by farmland. Đệ thought to himself, "Is this the same America I visited?" He was used to bigger cities when he studied in Cleveland and Baltimore. He also remembered Dr. Bui's description of their new home as "a wonderful fairy land!" Đệ said to himself, "I cannot trust Bui's perception of things!"

We were taken to Mr. D.'s restaurant where we were introduced to a few new people. Some ladies told me to come to them if I needed anything, to just consider them like my mother. Hearing this, tears came to my eyes because I missed my mother who was still trapped at home. I quickly took hold of myself because I did not want to be "weak" in front of my children.

After dinner, they brought us to our new house that Mr. Johnson had rented for us. It was a large house with four bedrooms and a good-sized living room and dining room. We had a large front yard and back yard. A beautiful flowering crabapple tree displayed its deep pink color outside the master bedroom. We also had flowering hydrangeas on our porch and fig and pecan trees in the back yard.

Mr. William Place was the mayor at the time, his wife was a nurse, and they owned a nursing home. They had two daughters, around our children's ages, who came to play with Miki and Kiti. We sent the children to Wilmot school during the summertime. Lily was fifteen at the time and had not finished elementary school. We taught her at home and asked the teacher to place her in fourth grade because of her size. Lily made some friends in her class.

Mr. Place recommended that we send some of our children to a private school out of town. It was Montrose Academy. Mimi was a good student there. She reported that sometimes her teacher would ask other students "How come Mimi was here for only two months and she can understand me better than you do?"

## FINDING MY BROTHER

After we were settled, my first goal was to find my brother Đích who was studying Economic Politics in Syracuse, New York. I told my husband to look for him. Đệ said, "How could we look for one person in an ocean of people? You only know his name and city, that's not enough!" I said, "If you cannot do this, I will find someone to help me and I am sure that Đích could be contacted." He challenged me as always.

I called up Mr. Place, told him about the situation, admitted that I did not know Đích's address, but I knew he had a scholarship to finish his Ph.D. in Economy in Syracuse. Mr. Place said that he would contact both American and Vietnamese personnel in New York to find out. It took a few days before Mr. Place gave me Đích's address and phone numbers. I found out that Đích had lost the American scholarship after the Vietnamese government collapsed. He said he had never felt so lonely among millions of people in New York. He wrote to the communist government in Việt Nam asking to return to Việt Nam to join his family there. The communist government told him that he would better serve the country by staying in the United States.

I told Đích to come to the Refugee's center and ask for help. They must have a humanitarian organization to help him now that he became a refugee, no longer an exchange student. He was given a job at a factory in New Mexico. From being a thinker, he now became a laborer. Besides screwing car doors in a factory, he also functioned as an adult foster care person and they gave him a manic, alcoholic old man to care for.

At first, he enjoyed his new job, making poems about his switching from being a bookworm to mechanics. He described his foster care man as "alternating between grandiose inflated self-esteem and sorrow and self-pity." But he retired early due to the jealousy and competition of his co-workers. He switched to investment, using his knowledge of economics and politics. He established a fund called "Self-Mastery Fund" and sold shares to his family members. This fund grew three hundred percent after eight years, averaging twenty-five percent interest each year.

## APPLYING FOR MY INTERNSHIP

Mr. D. and Mr. Johnson took me to the University of Arkansas, Little Rock. They talked with the Dean of the Medical School to secure me a position as an intern. Tivi was only one year old. When I practiced sending him to a babysitter nearby, I could hear him cry from my home. When I came in to check, I could see that he was scared of strangers and could not communicate to get his diapers changed. I felt sorry for him because he was so miserable in a strange house. Tivi was a good baby. He did not cry or rebel upon forced separation, but he looked very sad and scared. I felt that it was not good to let him stay with a babysitter at this age. I decided to stay home with him one more year before going to Little Rock to do my internship.

Little Rock was about five hours drive from home, so I stayed home taking care of my baby and studying for the Flex (Federal Licensure Examination) to practice medicine in the United States. I would take care of Tivi until the children returned from school.

One day, I opened the door for Đệ who came home for lunch. Tivi, who was two years old by now, followed behind. When Đệ came in, we were busy talking about what I cooked that day and what he had done in the clinic. When we sat down for lunch, I saw a woman carrying a small child coming walking toward our door from her car. I said, "Look at that woman, maybe her child is very sick, that's why she brings him here during your lunch hour!" I felt sorry for the woman and came to meet her at the door. I opened the door and asked, "What can I do for you?" before realizing that the baby in her arms was Tivi!

Tivi walked from her to stand by my side, when she asked, "Isn't he your son? I found him at the gas station and brought him here for you!" I was so embarrassed and surprised. We had not noticed that Tivi had left home when I opened the door earlier. We were so distracted by our own business that we missed him! I thanked the lady repeatedly for her kindness. I might have lost my baby if somebody else found him and kidnapped him. I would never forgive myself for this act of neglect.

"Why did you go out in the street by yourself?" I asked, realizing how lucky we had been. He beamed, "I go buy candies!" Wilmot was a very small community of about one thousand people. The road from our house to the gas station was very small with light traffic. Mostly people walked and children rode their bikes on this road. Tivi's sisters must have carried him out that way before to buy candy. At this age he must have thought he would just walk out, and people would give him candy! Thinking about it, we were very lucky that day, I am still thankful to the lady who saved my son.

A year later there was another funny and dangerous story that Tivi's sisters still tease him for. We were in Dallas, Texas, visiting our friend whose husband, Dr. Phan, was practicing pediatrics. While we were talking and the kids were playing downstairs, Tivi went upstairs by himself. We didn't realize he was upstairs until he came running down yelling "I bleed, mommy!" I ran toward him, and his upper lip was cut and bleeding badly. I put pressure on the wound and walked him to the living room. Đệ and Dr. Phan helped to place a band aid on the cut. When the bleeding had stopped, I asked Tivi what he was doing upstairs and he said, "I shaved my mustache!" Funnily, we did not have that kind of razor at home, but he had learned to imitate shaving from watching TV.

We stayed in Wilmot for about three years and went to at least four funerals of people we knew in this small community. First a priest died of a heart while raking leaves in his front yard. Then a young Vietnamese girl, died after she was sick for a few days. Then we had the shocking news that our sponsor, Mr. Johnson, died in his diving trip. Another man dropped dead in a friend's house when he was visiting at night. Some of our American friends recommended me to move to a larger city so that the children could benefit from visiting the museums, and larger libraries as it turned out we were thinking about leaving Wilmot.

At the beginning of 1977, I began my rotating internship at the University of Arkansas for Medical Sciences, Little Rock. I studied pediatrics and surgery in the main university and OB-GYN and Internal Medicine in a branch of the UAFMS in Pine Bluff, closer to home, about a four-hour drive. In both places, I lived in the dorm with much younger students. My family would visit during the weekend.

# CHAPTER XIX.

## MOVING TO MICHIGAN AND STARTING RESIDENCY IN PSYCHIATRY

I took and passed the Flex after I finished my internship in December 1977. Đệ joined the U.S. Air Force in January 1978. They promised to let him finish his OBGYN residency in the Air Force. Đệ was assigned to work at the Wurtsmith AFB, Oscoda, Michigan. On the day we moved from Arkansas to Michigan, it was snowing heavily. We rarely saw snow in Arkansas. We ran into a snowstorm when we reached the air force base. The snow was knee deep when we left our car to enter our new house at the base. The base was closed the next day due to the snowstorm.

Dr. T. was De's connection at the Air Force base. He told me that Đệ did not have to come to the hospital until nine each day. But everyday Đệ started to work at eight. He served there until July 1979. I had a few good experiences in Oscoda. I went ice fishing and smelting with a net and waders. I caught a lot of fish during these trips. I also went with a friend to a small town north of Michigan to pick mushrooms and watercress in the woods and along the creek banks.

## APPLYING FOR RESIDENCY

Around April of 1978, I began to apply for a residency in psychiatry. First, I went for an interview at the Metropolitan Regional Psychiatric Hospital in Westland, Michigan. This was advertised as the modernized version of the prestigious Eloise Hospital which was very old and very famous. In the hospital's complex, many multi-story buildings were condemned due to safety. Only one four-story building close to Michigan street was open for admission, outpatient, and in-patient services. Dr. B. was the Director of Training at the time.

I was taken on a tour of the hospital by Dr. B. and was introduced to other attending doctors including Dr. P, Dr. W, Dr. G, and Dr. S. After the interview, Dr. B. said he would contact me later regarding hiring.

My next interview was in Austin, Texas, at a state hospital. It was a large hospital with many buildings on campus. I was interviewed by six psychiatrists, members of staff. They were very nice and well organized. Some told me, "Come back and work with us." The director of training walked me around for a tour of the campus. I saw many clean and roomy houses with only a few staff and patients. I asked about the frequency of death and runaways. He said there were two deaths in the past year, one from suicide, the other possibly being killed. But they had a very large population of inpatients.

We later stopped by a Vietnamese restaurant in town. We met the owner who was also from Huế. I happened to know her mother. When I talked about my intention to come to Austin to work as a resident, she was not in favor. She said, "If uncle Đệ works in Michigan, you better find a position nearby. Texas is a long way apart. You should not make this sacrifice for your career. I've learned a sad lesson from my parents living apart!" I felt that she was right, and something might happen if we lived far from each other. I decided to stay in Michigan.

On our way home, Tivi got bored from the long drive. He started to whine. Đệ showed him an abandoned car on the side of the street and said, "Tivi, see that car, it cried and whined and that's why people left it there! They don't want to bring it home. Do you want Daddy to leave you there whining with the car?" Tivi immediately stopped crying. He identified fairly well with cars because he loved them. He recognized Mrs. D's car, a station wagon, when he was one and a half year old. At two and a half, he asked his father, after we had sold our first car, "Daddy, will our blue car come home and visit us?" And his first English sentence at age two was "Come to Shell for answer."

When we were back in Michigan, I got a letter from the state hospital in Austin offering me a position of first year resident in psychiatry. I hesitated for two weeks and did not respond to the Director of the Residency Training Program. At last, he called me and I apologized for my delay in responding to his letter. I thanked him for accepting me as a resident but told him my regret for not taking the position because my husband could not get permission to transfer from the Air Force.

The following week, Dr. B. from Metro Regional Psychiatric Hospital called and offered me the job. I told him about my interview in Austin and about their salary offer. Dr. B. offered me eighteen thousand dollars for the first year and my salary would be increased to thirty-five thousand the fourth year. I accepted the position and started my training on June 30, 1978, on Tivi's birthday.

## MY COLLEAGUES IN RESIDENCY

During the waiting period, I applied and obtained my license to practice in Michigan. When I started working, I was the only resident of the three-year program! Dr. B. told my supervisor Dr. S. to give me five to ten patients. About a week later, I had another classmate, Dr. L. Every morning, we had an hour of psychoanalysis from eight to nine given by a Ph. D. Other subjects were taught by our staff psychiatrist.

Dr. L. was a heavy-set woman with a radiant smile. She was quiet, deliberate, and somewhat slow. I noticed something different in her because she tended to shuffle. Her movements were sometimes stiff and heavy. Her slowness was not due only to her being overweight but also due to something else. I was intrigued by Dr. L.'s stance, gait, and facial expression.

She was always late for the morning lecture and the professor always waited for her. I frequently had to come to her office and remind her that the lecture started at eight. Sometimes we would wait for ten to fifteen minutes, and she would not show up. One morning, I came to her office to get her for the lecture, I found her kneeling on the floor. I called out, "Dr. L., let's go. The professor is waiting!" She signaled me to be quiet in a very religious way. When she was done with praying, I told her, "It is important for you to come because the professor would not start his lecture without you." She said, "No, praying is more important. I am killing my husband!"

I asked, "What? Why do you say so?" She said, "Because he was praying for me every night, he could not sleep at all, and he might die!" I ventured a question that I had wanted to ask many times earlier, "Are you taking any medication? What medicine that slows you down so much?" She confided" Promise me that you won't tell anybody. They will fire me. I am taking Haldol." I asked, "Why don't you take something for the side effects?" She said, "Yes, I also take Cogentin."

I felt sorry for her and kept her secret. Nobody suspected her illness. Three months passed by, and we had another first year resident, Dr. C. from the Philippines. After six months, we had two other residents, one from India and one from Korea. I was the only one who had the Flex and the Michigan license. My supervisor went on vacation and let me take care of her patients, about thirty people. The nursing staff would tease me, "You should be a staff psychiatrist. You don't need a supervisor! Now look at you, you are taking care of forty patients on your own for three weeks!"

When my supervisor came back, she assigned to me fifteen or sixteen patients, fifty percent more than the maximum allowed. All four residents started to take calls in rotation, and we had a staff back-up. I rarely consulted my back-up and the staff psychiatrist had trust in me. Dr. G., a Filipino lady, who was highly respected by nursing staff, told me, "Use your own judgment. You have good judgment." From that day on, I had more confidence in myself.

Dr. L. did not make progress in learning. She used to hire another resident to take calls for her. She would make the wrong diagnosis or give a diagnosis that did not exist in the book. She would argue with her patients and tell them that they lied. Sometimes she asked me to intervene to pacify her patients. Her supervisor began to see the problem and refused to supervise her. At the end of the first year, she left our hospital and was accepted as a resident in another psychiatric hospital in Michigan.

When I served the second year of residency, Dr. B. hired a third-year resident who was from India. He became our chief resident. He came to the hospital but did not work for the first few weeks because there was an error in his salary. In the papers, Dr. B. states his salary would be thirty-five thousand per year but in reality, the state paid him less. He continued to work but sued the state and he won. He criticized our psychoanalyst teacher who terminated his contract.

## MY EXPERIENCES IN RESIDENCY

We went to Lafayette Clinic to attend lectures weekly and prepare for the Psychiatric Board. During my eighteen months training at MRPH, one patient attempted suicide by hanging. One afternoon, we saw the police and many people gathered at the end of the small lake in front of the hospital. Apparently, somebody drowned. We looked at one another and one doctor cracked a morbid joke, "Whose patient was it? Who has the guilty conscience?" We all knew that our patients were locked up and we would not give anybody a pass without our supervisor's approval. But we still were scared!

One day, one of my patients was lost. She was a very beautiful Caucasian girl with blond hair and hazel eyes. She was about nineteen years old, mildly retarded, and very vulnerable. AT Staff took her on an outing without my permission. When they were about to return to the hospital, they could not find her and drove back without her. I learned this bad news late in the afternoon. I talked with the patient's social worker and both of us decided to go out looking for her after sending a message to the police and notifying her parents. We asked the AT staff where they last saw the patient and went there. We looked in all the bathrooms of that school and called out her name. We were afraid that she might have accidentally locked herself in the bathroom. After searching for half an hour without success, we returned to the hospital. Luckily, it turned out the police had found her walking on the street and brought her back.

I made a big mistake during my first year. A patient was brought in by the police wearing handcuffs and pleaded, "Doctor, can I get out of these cuffs. They bother me. I did not do anything wrong." I looked at the police officers and they gave no sign of objection. I nodded in agreement with taking off his handcuffs. As soon as the handcuffs were taken off, the patient jumped out the window and disappeared into the street. This was on the first floor and the patient did not get injured. Somebody told me that one time, the judge ordered a patient to be released from handcuffs during a hearing. The same thing happened, but on the fourth floor! The patient jumped out the window and broke many bones but did not die! From that day on, that particular judge stopped ordering release the handcuffs in his courtroom.

## TESTIFYING IN COURT

During my second year of residency, I had to testify in court in Detroit. I was told that a staff psychiatrist argued with the judge who requested the hospital to stop sending that doctor to court. I was asked to testify when a staff refused this job because he was not given enough time to examine the patients. I enjoyed going to court because it was a challenge for me. One time, I was given two or three extra new patients the day before we went to court. I worked overtime to interview the patients to gather necessary facts and history of their illness. Before interviewing the patient, we had to read to him the Michigan rules for civil commitment.

I used to testify for three to six patients during a court appearance. The hospital legal clerk would drive me to court, about thirty or forty minutes from work. I would share my concerns with the clerk about confusing one patient's history with another's. The clerk reassured me, "Don't worry, the minute you see the patient on the stand, you will remember everything about him, all his symptoms and history!" On the first trip, I asked her to describe what would happen in court and she said, "The lawyer would ask you to state your name, your license to practice, and where and when you examined the patient. Then you can give the judge a report about your findings and diagnosis. Be very down to earth, use easy simple terms that a six-year-old child can understand. Don't use psychiatric or medical jargons, the judge hates this." I said, "Then, it's not too hard!"

I asked the clerk what the judge would do after I testified. What if I did not understand what he said? She said, "The judge will mumble something that no one can understand. But I will know if he dismisses or commits the patient, that's all we need." She added, "Don't feel hurt if the judge dismisses a patient. That's not your fault and he will be responsible for his decision. You are through after testifying. The decision is up to the judge!"

Once I was sent to observe a jury trial for committing a manic female patient. Her lawyer came from New York and wanted to make a big name on the case. He was aggressive, arrogant, caustic, and sarcastic. The judge and the jury didn't seem to like him. Our staff psychiatrist who testified was calm, cool, and deliberate. The patient's lawyer even forbade him to refer to his notes. He told the judge, "Your honor, I think the doctor should not read his notes, he has to testify by memory!" The lawyer lost the case, and the patient was committed by the jury and the judge.

I learned a lot of common sense from other staff besides our staff psychiatrists. The admission staff, psychologist, nurses, and social workers helped me a lot. They would tell me who was expert on what to consult. One day I testified one manic patient and told the judge, "He was brought in the psychiatric hospital because two days ago, he took off these clothes, ran to a busy street corner, to direct the traffic. Then he tried to fight with the police when they intervened. When I interviewed him last night and told him about my duty to testify in court, and about whether it's up to the judge to release or commit him, he said, he was very happy to go to court to see the judge who will help him remarry his wife. He said he does not need to be in the hospital. He needs to get out to remarry his wife and direct the traffic."

I looked at the patient and told his story; he was very agreeable and looked at the judge, nodding his head. The judge could not help laughing and said, "I am impressed with the doctor's genuine testimony!" The clerk commented, "This is the first time that the judge laughed."

After eighteen months working at the Metro Regional Psychiatric Hospital, the state decided to close it down. Staff were moved to another hospital. This hospital mostly took care of long-term disabled elderly people. Most of them had dementia. All the residents were transferred to Northville Hospital.

I did my Child Psychiatry rotation for three months at Hawthorn Center. This is a famous facility working with child and adolescent psychiatric patients. Hawthorn Center was in Northville, Michigan. The ambience of this place was very friendly and relaxing. The ratio of staff to patients was high. All the patients and family received very good care once they were admitted to the facility. I thought that the name Hawthorn came from the principle of high staff to patient ratio, but I was told it got the name from the Hawthorn trees growing on the campus. The patients had an indoor heated swimming pool during wintertime. All staff were nice, friendly, and relaxed. My teachers at Hawthorn made me love working with children and adolescents.

After being transferred to Northville Hospital, I did my training in Neurology at a VA hospital near Detroit. My supervisor was Dr. Gandhi from India. He was an associate professor in Neurology and had taught me a lot. He was a staff back up when I was on-call but I never called him at night, only made a report to him in the morning. We attended a neurology grand round in a famous hospital in Detroit.

# CHAPTER XX.

## STARTING RESIDENCY IN CHILD AND ADOLESCENT PSYCHIATRY

After finishing my two years residency in adult psychiatry, I was accepted as a child and adolescent psychiatric resident at Hawthorn.

The Hawthorn staff was very selective and only trained one to three residents at a time. Many of my classmates also interviewed when MRPH was closed and were not accepted. I was transferred to Hawthorn from Northville Hospital in July 1980. Dr. W. was the director at the time. My supervisor was Dr. V.H. All my teachers at Hawthorn Center were very calm, friendly, mature, and knowledgeable. I felt very secure and happy working there.

Dr. W., who taught family therapy used to take the residents out for lunch or dinner after his lecture. At this one restaurant we frequented, we always had a good time. The owner would give a quiz sheet and any table who could answer correctly all ten puzzles would get free desserts for the group. Naturally, Dr. W. and our smart American residents would give all the correct answers.

I had nice memories and souvenirs from my time at Hawthorn Center. The good thing about Michigan M.H. policy was that they would not lay off employees in the middle of financial hardship. Employees would be partially laid off i.e., one week's layoff without pay here and there, and people were happy with this arrangement.

## MY YEARS OF PRACTICE

I graduated from Hawthorn in July 1982 and accepted my first job in Logansport, Indiana. It was at a Community Mental Health Center offering comprehensive in-patient, out-patient, partial hospitalization, and alcohol and drug counseling, among other services. We had about fifteen in-patient beds. Mental health care was still not strongly supported by the community, so we often had to go around introducing ourselves and making acquaintances. However, despite our efforts we still felt isolated and faced criticism. In my practice, I would treat acute patients and transfer long term psychotic ones to the state hospital which was unfortunately always short of staff. Unfortunately, I did not find the job rewarding due to these limited outcomes and I was not happy living further away from my family.

After nine months, I resigned and returned to Michigan to start private practice. In addition to private practice in G.B., Michigan, I also worked part time at Lapeer Community Mental Health Clinic. During this time, we later moved to Flint. My job in Michigan was more rewarding even though I did not make much money. I worked with two other private practitioners.

I observed an unfortunate trend from many of the patients that transferred to my practice. The patients gravitated towards the doctors who prescribed them minor tranquilizers for relaxation and assisted them in obtaining disability income.

One patient, whose doctor I was subbing in for, told me that his mother committed suicide with overdose, but he still was thankful to the doctor who provided him with valium and disability. For me, this kind of treatment relied solely on treating symptoms without addressing causes.

Another patient showed me her new Cadillac from the office window upstairs. She said, "You know, I got it for two months and I became disabled, and it was fully paid by my insurance!"

I asked, "Why are you disabled?" She said, "Because I was mad at my foreman and took a gun to work to shoot him. My son notified the foreman and took me to the hospital instead. I was hospitalized for one week and collected my disability income. I can't return to work and it's OK with me." Now she would see her doctor once month to get her valium and her new Cadillac paid off.

This kind of practice conflicted with my beliefs. I was the one who would try to wean the patients off sedative medication. For example, I treated a patient with an anxiety disorder that prevented her from driving or flying for six years. Her treatment included thorough psychotherapy and behavior modification for six months. But, with the help of her husband, she was able to resume her driving and she even drove to my office by herself in her last four sessions. She was very proud of herself for being able to function independently again, and afterwards her and her husband were able to enjoy a vacation in Hawaii! Through this I only gave her anxiolytic medication as a supplement to therapy for the first two months and weaned her off medication after four.

Because of these positive outcomes, I was distressed to find that the trend was moving towards fostering dependency. Maintaining consistent appointments and "easy" solutions due to high patient volume could sometimes provide a negative incentive to physicians. One of my colleagues even advised me, "Why do you have to wean off your patients? Give them some Valium and they will come every month!" I said, "Isn't it our goals to cure them and help them be independent? I would feel like a failure if they came back year after year becoming dependent on me!"

Perhaps he thought I was naive and stupid, but I didn't care, I just followed my own principle.

# CHAPTER XXI.

## RELOCATING TO OHIO

My husband felt that a career in OB-GYN would be hard as we grew older and he did not pursue it. He switched his interest to psychiatry instead. He left the US Air Force after serving for three years when he was accepted as a psychiatric resident at a hospital near Ann Arbor, Michigan. After the first year, his residency program was also closed. He applied and was accepted at Henry Ford Hospital in Detroit. After he finished his three years residency, he went to work out of state at a VA Hospital in Chillicothe, Ohio. It was around July 1984. He came home to Michigan every other weekend. I was planning to move to Ohio to be with him.

First, I went to work for two weeks at Cambridge State Hospital in Cambridge, Ohio. Besides mentally ill patients, they had a large population of MR patients on campus. When I walked around to visit patients in different buildings, I was given a friendly greeting by many patients. I asked Dr. T., one of my colleagues at Cambridge, how they knew my name. She replied, "They knew you by name before you came to Cambridge!" I appreciated the very warm welcome and acceptance.

They had a ward receiving patients with violent criminal histories, some were murder suspects that were acquitted by reason of insanity. The facility was understaffed and some patients had not seen a doctor for two weeks. I was given a list of seventy patients who needed to be seen and given progress notes. I tried to see everybody once or twice a week. Many patients were very kind and happy to finally talk to a doctor after so much delay. I was invited to stay for a permanent position, but unfortunately Cambridge was too far from Chillicothe to commute daily.

My next position took me to an opening at Scioto-Paint Valley Mental Health. Scioto and Paint were the names of two rivers in Chillicothe, Ohio. This town was a ninety-minute drive south of Columbus. I had a good time working at this place. In my second year, I received a raise of twelve percent and an additional fifteen percent in the third year. They had an effective policy of rating the physician's merit by the amount of time spent face-to-face with patients. During an eight-hour workday, I used to spend six or seven hours with the patients while reducing the paperwork. Another favored policy of the Scio-Paint Valley MHC was that if an employee did not take sick leave for two or three months, they accrued a personal day off. This would incentivize doctors to maintain their own health. These policies were very important in a profession where work-life balance and self-care were often difficult.

# CHAPTER XXII.

## MOVING TO LAS VEGAS, NEVADA

Las Vegas Adult Mental Health happened to expand in 1988 and they were recruiting psychiatrists. Đệ and I were already licensed to practice in Nevada since 1984. We wanted to move to Las Vegas to be close to our children who lived in Los Angeles.

We got our licenses on our way to visit our oldest daughter, Mimi, in California. Mimi had married and lived with her husband in Alhambra, California in 1983. Her brother, Kiki, also moved to Los Angeles to finish his college education. He had a job in LA county. Miki also joined Mimi after she finished high school in 1985.

Our children are very close to one another even though they fight sometimes. Following Mimi's example, the older ones practiced caring for their younger siblings at an early age. Although we always had live-in babysitters, our three oldest children would supervise them. When I complained about having "too many" children which impeded me from travelling as I desired, our oldest daughters, Mimi and Emmy, reassured me, "Don't worry Mommy. The three of us, including Kiki, will sponsor the three younger ones. You will have plenty of time to travel with daddy." And my younger children were very happy to have their sponsors besides Mom and Dad. That was why Miki automatically moved to California to be close to her "sponsor". Emmy also took care of Kiti who stayed with her family to finish medical school and continue to intern in Michigan. Tivi was supposed to follow his big brother, Kiki, but he preferred to go to Michigan to stay with Emmy's family. So, Emmy ended up sponsoring two younger siblings. Lily's family also lived nearby in Michigan.

I fostered this close relationship between siblings, thinking that they would have at least sixty years to support each other while we, the parents, only have fifteen to twenty more years of lucidity.

## PRACTICING IN LAS VEGAS

Dr. M. was the medical director at that time. He had recruited many psychiatrists for the new two-story hospital. Đệ started working at Southern Nevada Adult Mental Health Services (SNAMHS) in July 1988 and I joined him there in October the same year.

For the first four years, we went through three medical directors and an acting director. The last one, Director C., was manic with rather poor judgment. When we read his resume, it showed that he would hold at least two or three positions each year and would work in more than one place at a time. He never stayed longer than one or two years in any place. His resume was four or five pages long.

My husband made his diagnosis based on the candidate's professional resume. Đệ said, "His resume looks very similar to Dr. B's." Dr. B. was a psychiatrist with bipolar disorder. I was asked to treat Dr. B. as an inpatient when he was court committed. He was very intelligent but lacking tact and social skills. He repeatedly attempted to contact and talk to a distinguished lady in a meeting until he was sent to the hospital by a court order. Dr. B. had the same history of working many jobs at a time and moving around frequently. His resume was also five or six pages long.

This special Director C. would issue a memo threatening his colleagues' salaries if they took a vacation. He also threatened to report to the board if a colleague was sick and took leave. He would accuse doctors of abandoning their patients due to their own sickness. Other departments such as nursing and social work also suffered from his creative attempt at revamping the system.

He seemed to believe in his misguided initiatives often claiming that we were, "under my new regime." Some staff told me, "He is turning the whole place upside down! He is turning nursing staff into secretaries and secretaries into slaves!"

He also had conflict with a patient who threatened his life and his family's. He was scared and asked for protection from the staff for a while. Each time he sent out a memo, a mental health IV technician working in my team would say "Dr. C. is crazy! Send this memo to the governor!"

Despite this, he was nice to me and my husband. He asked me to interview the candidates who applied for jobs at the hospital. But when these candidates saw his memos, they promised to come but never did. He told my husband, "You are the only one who pitches in to help me with my new plan!"

However the effects of his mismanagement were becoming clear, most of the psychiatrists at SNAMHS either retired, resigned, or transferred to other state facilities. My husband ended up leaving to work with the correctional system, and I went to Southern Nevada Child and Adolescent Services starting July 1992.

## ATTEMPTED ROBBERY

In one of our early years in Vegas, we almost got kidnapped and robbed in our own garage. On Christmas eve, on our way home from a Chinese restaurant in town, we were followed by two robbers. We still did not know where and when they started following us. When my husband parked the car in the garage, I walked around to take a package out of the trunk, when suddenly a tall skinny young man entered the garage.

He followed me to the door while I walked between the two cars and said, "Get in the house!" As my husband unlocked the door and pushed it ajar, I called out, "Honey, look at this boy! He wants to follow us!" At that time, I noticed that he had a gun in his right hand.

He held it loosely by the handle and it had no trigger. He waved the gun up and down and said in a very soft voice "Get in the house." Đệ looked back when I called him. He saw the man with the gun and immediately turned around and walked toward him. I was waiting for our burglar alarm to go off. I also believed that the gun was fake or not working. Now, he was waving the gun in De's face as he continued to say, "Get in the house."

He did not look straight at us his eyes mostly shifted down while he waved the gun. I thought to myself, "This is a novice. He does not know how to threaten people!" While waiting for the alarm signal, I tried to bargain with him. "No, I don't want to get in the house now. I want you to go home first." He then changed his strategy and said, "Close the garage door" in a very low voice, without eye contact. He looked tired and weak, not active, or aggressive. I thought about blocking his arm and taking away the gun, but I feared that during the struggle, the gun might fly off and damage our new cars. I only told him, "No, I don't want to close the garage. I don't know how! You better go home."

By this time, a younger teenager descended from their car and joined us in the garage. There was a heavy iron hammer at the side of our garage door, below the garage's opening button. I moved to stand between covering the weapon and garage opening button with my back. I hoped the two robbers would not see them. The first one told the second one, "Close the garage door." But he did not know the mechanism to do it.

Finally, our alarm began to sound. The chief robber asked, "What is it?" I lied, "I don't know." I shook my head. Then the alarm signal sounded louder and louder. The robber repeated his question "What is it?" and I lied again, "I don't know." My husband was more honest and charitable. He did not want the young men to be confronted by the police who were supposed to come when the alarm goes off. He said, "It is the alarm. The police are coming. You better go home." The robbers slowly and deliberately walked out of the garage, entered their car, and drove away.

We looked at their car and tried to identify it. Đệ knew the make and color of the car. He remembered what the robbers were wearing. I guessed their height and weight. We both knew the robbers' races but disagreed about their ages. Đệ thought they were about twenty-six and eighteen. Working with children and adolescents, I guessed that the older one was about seventeen or eighteen and the younger thirteen or fourteen years old, and I was right.

The police came and made a report. Đệ gave him the information about the robbers. Two days later, a police detective called us and reported that they were caught. The police identified their stolen car parked outside when they were at a party. The police went to arrest them at the party. I asked the detective about their handgun, "Was it real or fake?"

She said, "It was real, but it did not work without a trigger." The detective arranged a day for us to testify in court. I asked what the charge against them was. She said, "Attempt to kidnap with a deadly weapon and attempted robbery and robbery, car theft, etc..." She added, "They had robbed two other victims, one before and one after you!"

When we went to court, we met the other victims. One was a young pizza delivery man. He was driving his wife's car when he was followed by these two robbers while leaving an apartment complex. With the threat of the gun, they made him enter his car. The older sat behind him with the gun. The younger sat in front. The older ordered him to give his watch and wallet to the younger one. Then they made him drive to a deserted street, told him to stop and leave his car. Then the robbers drove away.

The other victims were a couple, Mr. and Mrs. B. They drove home after watching a movie with their seventeen-year-old daughter. They saw their garage door open, and a strange car parked in there with the hood facing the street and the trunk open. The robbers had their T.V., videotape recorder, video camera, jewelry, etc... in the garage. They were in the process of loading the stolen items into the trunk.

Mr. B. said he wanted to park in front of his garage to block the robber's way out. But his daughter was panicking and told him to drive away. Mr. B. drove past his garage and parked. He opened the door and was about to walk in to confront the robbers. Mrs. B. and their daughter were hysterical because they saw the taller robber stop his activity and point the gun toward them. They told him to get back in the car and wait for the robbers to drive away. This happened the same night they attempted to rob us just two hours later and ten miles away.

When we testified in court, the older robber looked like a college student while wearing glasses and a suit. He must have gained about twenty pounds during his two months of confinement. He looked like a very nice young man, and I could hardly recognize him. But I remembered his color, his height, and eyeglasses.

I told the judge how I lied to the robbers three times, claiming that I did not know how to close the garage door or recognize the sound of the alarm. I also told the judge that our robber was soft spoken and did not swear or threaten. Remembering the compassion my mother showed when we confronted the mother of the robber so many decades ago I added that I hoped that he would stop his criminal lifestyle and if he was incarcerated would not learn more criminal ways from the other convicts.

Since this aborted robbery, we were more cautious. We would immediately close the garage after we parked. We would look before opening the door and never open it even for boy and girl scouts coming to sell their candies/cookies because you never know who a criminal could be.

## RETIREMENT

After my transfer to Children Behavioral Services, my work was not as challenging thanks to the support I received from the staff. My supervisor was also nice and understanding. I had made some friends among nursing staff, clinicians, and secretarial staff. My friends at work made my life fuller and my work easier. I was nominated "Employee of The Year" and "Distinguished Woman in Southern Nevada" in 1993 and 1995.

After a long and fulfilling career, I could not wait to retire in 1997 so that I could travel and visit the world as I desired and as encouraged by my husband and children. I was happy to work for the state of Nevada. We are happy to live in Las Vegas, the World Center for Entertainment. I wrote a poem about Las Vegas and its Casinos to invite our friends from all over the world to come and visit.

Lastly, I want to quote a poem which Miki wrote when she came to Wilmot, Arkansas and began to learn English "America is the best. Where people can play, and rest."

# EXHIBIT A

My father was a teacher, poet, and a freelance musician. He wrote beautiful poems to celebrate the teachers and pupils. He made sentimental songs to celebrate his father-in-law's seventieth birthday. He taught his students to sing and dance and perform during celebrations. My maternal grandfather loved him a lot. He was also the favorite of my maternal aunt, the late Emperor Khải Định's second wife.

My father loved to study Chinese characters and French phonetics. He had a few French teachers and friends who were close. They would discuss French poetic literature and Vietnamese culture. I remembered when Mr. Dufrene and LeBris would come to our house for dinner. They loved my mother's cooking and Vietnamese food.

It was thanks to this relationship that my father could save my sister's brother-in-law's life, by talking with his French teacher and friends. My sister's brother-in-law was caught with many more Vietnamese youths who were given a death sentence by the French authority. This happened in the late 1940's when the French returned to power in Việt Nam.

# EXHIBIT B

My sister Khánh Trợ happened to be teaching the daughter of a famous chef. This chef was serving the French General who lived in Huế at the time.

She discussed the need to save Chị Hoa's nephew, Hà, with the chef. She talked about how Hà's grandmother had received a certificate award titled, "Your Virtue as a Widow and a Mother Deserves Commendation" (Tiết Hạnh Khả Phong) from the late King. This meant that Hà came from an excellent family.

The chef introduced my sister to the General to ask for mercy for Hà and the French General gave the order to release him.

# EXHIBIT C

During my years in junior high school, I frequently spent summer days at my teacher Phan's house, Teacher Phan had two daughters and four sons. His oldest daughter was Chieu, my classmate. I was close to all of them, even the baby boy Chuong, six or seven years old at the time. Chuong used to get a candy bar when Mrs. Phan returned from the market. He would call me out and offer me a bite.

Teacher Phan had a good-sized library. I used to read French novels and drama with Chieu and one or two other classmates who came for the reading. I would be the translator and Chieu was assigned to look up difficult words in the dictionary. I sometimes would guess the meanings based on the context before letting Chieu read it aloud from the dictionary. My guesses would be right about fifty percent.

I always stayed the whole day at teacher Phan's house and ate lunch with the family. Sometimes they invited me to stay longer for dinner and I would stay if it was not too late. I would ride my bike home before dark. When we were tired of reading, I would join in singing with Chieu's brothers and their friends. They formed a group playing music and Kha was the guitarist. I had a good time during my teenaged years with teacher Phan's family and always felt loved and welcome.

Chieu sat next to me in class. She was very good at memorizing the lessons which she would recite out for me to write down when we had a test. Sometimes teacher Huong (who was my cousin's husband) suspected this conspiracy. He would stand by my side and Chieu had to stop reciting. I would continue to write about my own ideas to dissipate his suspicions. Chieu and I made a good team. I would help her out with math and languages. Some classmates said that I was favored by the teachers, and I believed they were right in some respects. In needle work and drawing, when somebody especially Đăng Nga, was not satisfied with her work, she would give her work to me. When I put my name below it, I would get a better grade than the owner's favorite work.

All my teachers were nice, but nobody was so close to the students as teacher Phan. He was a poet and a writer. He beautifully translated famous Vietnamese poems into French ones. He taught the students free of charge and gave them treats. Teaching was his hobby. I miss him a lot.

# EXHIBIT D

During my last three years in high school, I used to live with my friend Doan Thi Dong's family. Dong's mother was from the Viceroy's family and she was Đệ's cousin. Dong's father was the high school accountant, Mr. Doan Tú Thanh. I considered him my teacher and respected and loved him a lot. He was not rich, but he would welcome any relative or students who came to live with him. Naturally, Dong's mother was very nice and warm, friendly, and loving. But the chief of the family had to be very generous and altruistic to raise so many teenagers, at least six of them, under his roof!

I always felt welcome, loved, and respected by Dong's family. I recall that we always had boiled hand shredded Bok choy dipped in shrimp sauce, mixed sautéed vegetable with pork and shrimp, bowls of soup, and a fish dish. At lunch, we used to save the fish dish for dinner. Teacher Doan impressed me with his generosity, politeness, and sense of humor. He was always pleasant, always smiling, and telling nice jokes. Teacher Doan had for his family a large room in Khải Định High School.

In my twelfth grade, our bedroom at teacher Doan's place was situated next to our classroom. Each morning or afternoon class hour, I just opened the back door, which connected to my classroom, and entered the room from the back while my classmates were standing up to greet the teacher coming from the opposite door.

I have seen in teacher Doan the calmness and happiness of a loving family life where all members of the family lived in harmony and affection. Later in life, I wanted to have an opportunity to tell him how much I appreciated and respected him.

When I decided to do this, either in a letter or in person, I learned the news that he had passed away. It was in his memory and teacher Phan's that I had opened two teacher's funds to honor their name.

I still remember teacher Doan's joke when he learned that Đệ wanted to marry me, "Anh Đệ really has the guts to ask for Chị Phùng Mai's hand!"

Still to this day tears come to my eyes when I think about my two beloved and respected teachers. I composed my first Chinese poems to express my love and gratitude toward them. These poems were written in Chinese characters by a famous scholar in Toronto, Canada, Professor Thuy Quoc. They were published in a Public Works Letter in 1994. I am still suffering an unresolved grief from the losses of my teachers. I thought they would wait for me to say good-bye!

# EXHIBIT E

Working at SNAMHS could be a challenging experience. We were in teams composed of a psychiatrist, a psychologist, a social worker, and a mental health IV technician. When I first came, we had an admitting unit where two or three psychiatrists took turns to evaluate and treat the patients. When the patient was more stable, that is less psychotic, not agitated, or aggressive, he would be transferred to the new hospital to be treated by other psychiatrists.

I used to interview the patients in the admission unit with a mental health IV technician present in the interview room. One of the technicians would say, "This is what we expected from a psychiatrist!" when he saw me listening and interacting with the patient. I was surprised at the technician's comment, but I later found out that some psychiatrists would have a "personality conflict" with the patient that would lead to aggravation.

After one year the policy changed, and we would take turns to directly admit new patients to the hospital. We had eight units in the new hospital. Each team had a case load from ten to twenty patients. If a team treated the patients and families effectively, they could be discharged in a short time and the case load would be less heavy. My team used to have below ten patients at a time because we would take a calculated risk when we evaluated the readiness of patients for discharge. Naturally, we would spend more time with the patients and family to analyze and study each case. We would ask the family, patient, and ourselves what was the worst things that could happen if the patient is released before we release him.

One funny thing happened in my team around 1990 or 1991. One day, we admitted a new patient who was a Việt Nam veteran. He was average, not quite psychotic, not severely disturbed.

When he saw me, he pointed at me and said, "I saw this doctor before, somewhere!" The IV technician laughed "No, you haven't. This is the first time that I introduce you to Dr. C! Sit down." The patient would not sit down and affirmed, "Yes, I saw her in the news or a magazine. I knew her!" The technician said, "No, you are delusional!"

The patient continued, "Yes, I saw her shaking hands with General Westmoreland, standing by a chopper or a small airplane, in the news!"

The technician laughed louder "No, now you're hallucinating!" meaning that he was seeing things which were not there. I felt sorry for the patient being labelled as psychotic.

Suddenly, I remembered a photograph years ago with a General W. Dr. Dolbee took this picture when General W. stopped by B'Lao Airport to visit us. I was told, "This is a big event! You need to go with me to the airport and meet General W!" Afterwards, Dr. Dolbee gave me the picture as a souvenir. I showed this picture to an American friend to see if she recognized the officer, and she replied, "Yes! That is Westy!"

I later told the patient, "Yes, you are right. I did shake hands with General Westmoreland." I showed the picture, "You are not delusional or hallucinating!" The technician opened her mouth in surprise, "Then it is true, Dr. C. I thought that he was making things up!" And she apologized to the patient.

Phùng Mai T. CôngTằng 1940s

Phùng Mai T. CôngTằng 1950s

1960s, Phùng Mai T. CôngTằng, husband Đệ Dat Ton with first three children (left to right) Mimi, Kiki, and Emmy

Phùng Mai T. CôngTằng 1950s

# ABOUT THE AUTHOR

Dr. CôngTằng Tôn Nữ Phùng Mai was born in Huế, Việt Nam on January 14, 1932, to an aristocratic family who were descended from Emperor Minh Mạng, the second emperor of the Nguyễn dynasty (reigned 1820-1839).

She studied in Huế eventually completing her medical studies before working alongside her husband at Huế Hospital. In Việt Nam, she would continue to open a private practice and lecture at the University before relocating to the United States in 1975 where she would continue medicine before transitioning to adult and adolescent psychiatry. After relocating to Las Vegas, she continued working at Southern Nevada Adult Mental Health Services (SNAMHS) before opening her own private practice.

After years of psychiatric practice, she retired and dedicated her efforts to charitable works in Las Vegas and Việt Nam, continuing the spirit of her sister, the eminent Bhikkhuni Trí Hai (Tam Hy).

With her husband, Đệ Dat Tôn, she has seven children, ten grandchildren, and three great-grandchildren.

She is the author of "The Book of My Life," her memoirs that span a lifetime of over 90 years, two continents, and two careers. This is the first edition of this work, and more chapters are being written every day. She currently lives in Las Vegas, Nevada.

Made in the USA
Las Vegas, NV
21 May 2024